#3
990
D1791070

PROJECTS FOR
YOUNG SCIENTISTS

COMPUTER SCIENCE

BY ALLEN L. WOLD

FRANKLIN WATTS
NEW YORK | LONDON | TORONTO | SYDNEY | 1984

TO MY WIFE, DIANE,
FOR MAKING THIS ALL POSSIBLE

Photographs courtesy of Hewlett-Packard Company:
opposite p. 1, pp. 5, 42; Wang: p. 15;
Tandy Corporation/Radio Shack: pp. 22, 54;
IBM: p. 49; Apple Computer, Inc: p. 60, 79;
Atari, Inc.: p. 84; Bell Labs: p. 102.

Library of Congress Cataloging in Publication Data

Wold, Allen L.
Computer science.

(Projects for young scientists)
Includes index.
Summary: A guidebook for the student who wants to use a computer in a science project, indicating the ways computer knowledge can be used in the performance of an investigation or project or in the analysis of the results.
1. Science—Experiments—Data processing—Juvenile literature. 2. Microcomputers—Juvenile literature.
(1. Science—Experiments—Data processing.
2. Microcomputers. 3. Experiments. 4. Computers.
5. Programming (Computers)) I. Title. II. Series.
Q163.W64   1984   502'.854   83-23572
ISBN 0-531-04764-4

Copyright © 1984 by Allen L. Wold
All rights reserved
Printed in the United States of America
5 4 3 2 1

CONTENTS

CHAPTER 1
BEFORE YOU BEGIN
1

CHAPTER 2
INFORMATION
MANIPULATION
13

CHAPTER 3
NUMERICAL
CALCULATION
20

CHAPTER 4
DATA AND ITS ANALYSIS
28

CHAPTER 5
COMPUTER GRAPHICS
36

CHAPTER 6
PICTORIAL
REPRESENTATION
44

CHAPTER 7
GRAPHS AND CHARTS
58

CHAPTER 8
SIMULATION
AND MODELING
64

CHAPTER 9
COMPUTER CONTROL
OF OTHER DEVICES
82

CHAPTER 10
COMPUTER SOUND
88

CHAPTER 11
INSIDE THE COMPUTER
92

CHAPTER 12
ODDS AND ENDS
100

CHAPTER 13
PUTTING IT ALL TOGETHER
108

INDEX
120

COMPUTER SCIENCE

PROJECTS FOR YOUNG SCIENTISTS

1
BEFORE YOU BEGIN

This is not a book for beginning computer programmers. It will not tell you how to use a computer, *per se*, nor will it tell you how to program one. Instead, it is intended as a guidebook for the junior high or high school student who wants to use a computer in a science project. It assumes that you already know at least the rudiments of computer programming.

Even if you know quite a bit about how a computer works, it may not be immediately clear to you how a computer can be applied to the scientific field of study you are interested in. Or, your main area of interest might not be one of the traditional scientific disciplines or branches of technology at all. Yet even the social sciences and the humanities can provide science project subjects—with the help of a computer.

A computer can be used in almost any area of study. If you haven't yet decided on a project, this book should give you some ideas. It will indicate to you some of the ways you can use your computer knowledge in the performance of your investigation or experiment or in the analysis of the results of your project.

Even if you don't use a computer in the project itself, you can use one in the presentation of your project results or to display what you have learned. Preparing a good display has value in itself, and a computer's graphics and sound capabilities can be of great help in giving your presentation a feeling of professionalism and competence.

If you have no good project ideas of your own, it may be possible to collaborate with a friend who does have one, especially if he or she can see the need for a computer but is unfamiliar with computers, or not very skilled in their use. You can provide the computer expertise necessary, and, at the same time, demonstrate other skills that are essential in any real research effort—those of cooperation and coordination of ideas and goals.

WHY USE A COMPUTER?

There are two complementary reasons why you might want to use a computer in your science project.

The first is that the computer can actually help you perform the experiment. It can help in the analysis of the results or the solution of mathematical problems, or it can form a part of the display of those results or of the project itself, regardless of the scientific discipline or subject of the project.

The second reason is that although computers are fascinating in themselves, and computer science can be the subject of a project, you may be looking for something else to do with the computer other than demonstrate your knowledge of computer science.

Computer science is different from most other forms of science, which are largely investigative. That is, one looks at the world and tries to figure out, by the scientific method, why and how the world works the way it does. Computer science has this aspect, too. But because the computer is a man-made device, a product of technology rather than a natural phenomenon, even computer projects of an investigative nature will be different from those in other disciplines.

This is not to deny that there is true science in the investigation of the principles of electronics and materials that enable computers to be designed and built, or in the discovery of theories used to create and control computers. But projects exploring computer science will, for the most part, be more demonstrative than investigative.

Therefore, this book will be different from other books on science projects, since most of the projects we suggest will assume that you are interested in integrating two different fields of study, the subject of the project and computer science.

For those of you whose interest lies in any of the traditional sciences or the social sciences, you will use a computer to augment or supplement your project rather than just be your project. You will still have to know, or learn, quite a bit about computers to be able to make good use of them in performing your experiment, analyzing your data, and especially in creating a good display.

But if your primary interest is computer science, you will find plenty of suggestions for how to show your knowledge and expertise in a wide variety of areas. Chapter 11, in particular, discusses topics devoted to how the computer works, and many of the topics in other chapters will give you some ideas on how to demonstrate the computer itself, how to explore some of its limits and potentials. Taking a cue from any of the subjects mentioned, you can design a project that is not only scientific in its own right but which also serves to exemplify computer control, graphics, data handling, number-crunching ability, or whatever. Though we do not stress computer science used alone, it is the core of this book, and if you pursue computer science as a career, you will almost certainly find yourself trying to solve similar problems in the real world.

A good computer scientist, after all, needs to know about the application to which his or her computer system or software will be put. Computers do not function in isolation. We use them and the programs that control them to do things, to work for us, to help us solve problems. Thus, one extremely important consideration is to show how computers relate to the rest of the world. To this end, this is a book of ideas that can be explored to demonstrate how computers can be used in real-world situations and applied to real-world problems.

Computers are interesting in and of themselves, but unless we can relate them to our lives, and to the larger world around us, they are nothing more than toys. Even if your primary interest is the study of computer science, you should remember that even that has, as its ultimate goal, the production of more powerful and useful tools for research, for developing our technology, and for improving our daily lives.

WHICH COMPUTER?

Though some students may have access to large computers and expensive peripherals, the computer most of you will be using will be a microcomputer, such as an Apple, a PET, a TRS-80, an Atari, or even one of the smaller home computers that are now widely available, such as the VIC-20, the Timex/Sinclair 1000, or the TI-99/4A.

The projects suggested in this book are not intended for any particular make or model of computer. Some of the ideas here will work on only the larger machines, or only with the addition of extra equipment. And, since different computers vary greatly in their ability to produce color graphics or sound, projects that make use of those capabilities might not be possible on your machine at all.

A few projects, if they were to be fully developed or explored, would require resources unavailable to most students. Some will require more than an elementary knowledge either of the topic itself or of the computer. All will require that you take the time and have the ability to do research. But by the time you have finished reading this

Computers do not function in isolation.
We use them and the programs that
control them to help us solve problems
in the real world.

book, you should have an idea for a project within your reach and be thinking about how to organize your investigation.

NO ROBOTICS HERE

There is no hard and fast division between the various aspects of computer use in a science project. Almost every project that makes use of a computer will involve some computer science, the use of computer hardware, the exploration of a computer's limits, as well as the analysis and manipulation of data, the construction of a model, the solution of mathematical problems, or the use of computerized displays. But any one project will probably emphasize one aspect over the others.

This book will give computer hardware only a passing reference. If you are a hardware hacker, or an electronics hobbyist, there are plenty of other books that can help you. There are several kits available, for those who want to build their own computer but would rather not start from scratch. There are also texts to help you design and build your own special peripherals and interface cards.

Robotics is a subject of such complexity that it can be discussed here only in the most superficial way. Again, there is plenty of other material available, both in kit and text form, to help you with this, though we will mention several areas where computer control of peripherals and of other devices might be used to demonstrate some of the more elementary principles of robotics.

Hardware projects would, of course, make good science fair exhibits, and demonstrations of the intricacies of robotics and the computerized control of machines, remote sensing, and so on, offer excellent opportunities for research and experimentation. Such exhibits are fascinating to watch and worthwhile to develop. But that is another whole area of computer science—computer technology, really—and we leave that to others to guide and help you.

THE COMPUTERIZED DEMONSTRATION

Using a computer can help your science fair project considerably, but it will also demand additional work on your part. This additional work can make the difference between a merely good project and an excellent one.

There is no sense using a computer in a science project unless the computer will actually improve the project in some way. There are plenty of good books on how to design, prepare, and present a science project, but including a computer in your plans will add another whole dimension to your undertaking.

Using a computer with a project in another discipline implies that your abilities and interests are broader than the single subject you chose to investigate. Intelligent and imaginative use of a computer in such a project will indicate the difference between a mere technician and someone with the potential to design and manage important research projects in the real world.

To take the best advantage of the computer's abilities, the computer and your competence in using it must be considered at the very start, while planning the project itself. This means deciding how a computer can be used in the running of the project, how to collect your data so that it can be used by a computer for analysis, how to take advantage of a computer's number crunching or graphics capabilities, and so on. One of the major ways a computer can help will be in its ability to provide a dynamic display of many aspects of your work.

A science project on the effect of fertilizer on bean plants, however well designed and executed, will just sit there. In contrast, a science project on principles of mechanics should move. Even more, if the computer is part of the display, it should make use of the machine's special features and not just show results on a screen.

A computer is dynamic. It is a device that does things. When people see a computer in action in a demonstration, it becomes the focus of their attention. They expect it to do more than just print text. In this way (among others), using a computer can make your project different from most other projects.

THE SELF-OPERATING PROGRAM

Your computer display should be self-operating. Although you should be present to prevent misuse of the computer, and to answer questions pertinent to the demonstration, you should not sit at the terminal and run the program. This obscures the observer's view and also indicates that you haven't designed your project or display well enough to run by itself.

When the program has finished, rather than your having to type **RUN** again, it should start over automatically. On the other hand, it should not just cycle through if no one is watching. There should be a prompt on the screen, telling the observer how to start the demonstration. There should also be prompts, whenever the program pauses, to let the observer exit the program if he or she desires.

If possible, the program should be interactive, so that the observer can make things happen. This is one of the strongest features of computerized instruction, and one of the most important aspects of any computer display. By including prompts, or perhaps a menu, you can involve the observer directly in your discovery or demonstration. To do this successfully, you will have to design error-trapping routines, so that incorrect or mischievous entries will not cause your program to crash.

In other words, besides computer use and the topic of your project, you should also demonstrate some facility in the area of human/machine interfacing. Even if your spectators just watch what happens on the screen, your display should be designed so that the viewer's comfort and ability to grasp the material is given full consideration. If the computer forms only a background for your project, and is not part of the display, this consideration will be less important but should not be overlooked.

TO DEMONSTRATE AND INFORM

Your computer display should be both demonstrative and informative. "Demonstrative" means that not only does the computer do something, it also shows how that something was done. A computer should not be used simply to replace a poster, photograph, or other illustrative material. A computer display can move and change, and that facility should be made use of, whether by program control or by observer interaction. Even a computer display of text can be made active instead of passive.

A program that merely accesses disk files, without showing how, is not very interesting, though you might use disk access in some particular aspect of your project. If disk access is the subject you are exploring, then your demonstration should show how it was done and why it was done that way. A program that calculates a very large number, beyond the precision of your computer, could be an interesting piece of work, but if the computer just shows the number, without demonstrating the computer's limits and how you transcended them, the display will not be interesting.

"Informative" simply means that after the program has run, the observers, given normal intelligence, should know more than when they came. But you should take special care here not to assume prior knowledge on the part of the observer, either of how a computer works, about the subject of your research, or why your results are important. Besides information on how your project was run and its results, you should also provide sufficient background material so that someone unfamiliar with your topic will not be confused or overwhelmed with strange jargon.

Even if your interest is not primarily computer science, you should provide information on how the demonstration program works. This may be in the program itself, if possible or appropriate, or it may be by means of supplementary materials, such as a flowchart or diagram. This will enhance the quality of the display as well as its informativeness.

Although it is impossible to anticipate all the questions an observer might ask about the content, significance, or demonstration of your project, as much as possible should also be included in your computerized display. This information will probably be of only the most fundamental or basic nature, being supplemented by a written report, but the higher the information content of your display, the more attention it will get.

MORE THAN AN EXERCISE

Your display—and your project—should not be trivial. That is, it should not be a mere exercise, such as might be done by someone less experienced than you. It should be something that has required some genuine effort on your part, rather than a project taken out of a book or magazine and copied to perfection. Depending on your age and the amount of knowledge with which you start, there is a broad range here.

A program that displays the observer's name a hundred times on the screen might be trivial for a senior who has been programming for three years, but for a ninth-grader who has just learned to program, it could be a very interesting demonstration of some of the basic abilities of the computer. This is especially true if the program not only prints the name but also shows how it accepts a name from the keyboard, stores it in a variable, controls the screen to print the name, counts the number of times the name is printed, and shows how the program recycles back to the beginning again.

No matter what discipline you choose for your project, your computerized display should reflect the sophistication and degree of effort that went into creating it. The display should be imaginative in that it not only demonstrates your project or its results but also shows why you chose to supplement or augment your display with a computer, or why you used a computer to help you in the execution or solution of your project. The most successful investigation into voting habits in your neighborhood, presented as a simple table, could just as well have been displayed on a poster. An understanding of the evolution of stars, given simply as text, would not justify displaying that text on a computer's screen.

SUPPLEMENTARY MATERIALS

Unless your project is in computer science itself, the programs you write will be additional to your main work. Whether the programs are the subject of the project, or supplementary to it, they should be well designed as programs and clearly understandable to other people. You should make every effort to write the best program you know how.

This doesn't mean that you have to stretch to produce a highly sophisticated or "clever" program. Your project doesn't have to be used as a text for teaching programming. But you should do your best to use good programming style and good programming methods, and to make good use of your computer's special capabilities. Your program should be one that you can be proud of in and of itself, aside from what it does.

You might want to supplement your program with a flowchart, a listing, and documentation. If your project is strictly computer science, these will be very important, and you should pay considerable attention to their production. If the program is supplementary to another project, such additional material is less important, but it can be helpful in explaining how you did what you did.

The flowchart should be well drafted and drawn on a large, separate card. Each step should be carefully labeled, perhaps with more detail than you would use in preparing a flowchart for your own use. Especially if the program is interactive, the observer should be able to follow what the program does when he or she responds to prompts.

Your program listing should be as attractive as you can make it, without letting its looks override its usefulness. Indentations within indentations several layers deep can make a listing harder to read, not easier. Comments should be clearly delineated, with modules and subroutines clearly labeled.

And although there should be documentation embedded within the listing, as comments, you should also have a more complete explanation of how the program works, carefully typed. As examples, examine the program explanations that appear in computer magazines. This separate documentation helps keep the listing clean and should be as complete and thorough as possible.

To further improve your display, you can provide illustrations of logic circuits, photographs of the inside of the computer, or other supporting materials. You may also want to have diagrams to show how different peripherals were used. Consider carefully, however, how much of such extra material is needed. Your aim is to make the project completely intelligible to the observer. Additional materials can help explain how the program works, and why that particular task was a good subject for a science project, but they should not take the place of a good computerized display.

2
INFORMATION MANIPULATION

Today, computers are used most extensively in the field of data processing. It may not seem that the methods and techniques used to prepare phone bills, bank statements, and inventories can have much use in a science project, but that is not the case. Data processing is a term that covers many specialized computer uses, some of which are purely practical, others of which have interesting implications in areas such as artificial language.

Remember, data processing simply means the manipulation of information. Information can come in many forms, such as names, addresses, and numbers through the entire texts of stories, complete records of motor vehicle accidents, and tables of physical data for insect growth.

Information manipulation usually requires that the data to be worked on be stored in a data file, although data statements in a BASIC program can be used if the amount of information is not too great. The two methods of data storage each has its advantages and disadvantages.

To use a data file, a program to create, edit, and access it must first be written. This is not easy, but the language COBOL was created just for this purpose. The advantage to using data files is that the program manipulating the data can be separate from the one that enters data into the file, can be quite short, and can access any number of different files, as long as the information within each file is in the same format. Also, not all the data has to be contained in memory at the same time, but can be called up from storage—disk or tape—as it is processed.

On the other hand, data statements within a BASIC program take up many lines of code in the listing and must sometimes all be loaded into the memory at once, which can occupy a lot of RAM. In compensation, data statements are easier to write, and they don't need a data file management program. Also, they are not subject to the same kind of keyboard entry errors as those that can occur when producing a file, and they can be easily edited.

By means of a data file, or data statements within a program, you can access the same information over and over again for repeated operations. The computer will not only perform the desired manipulations and display the results, but it can also, with the proper program instructions, demonstrate what those manipulations were.

ALL THAT DATA

If you are an amateur astronomer, you are probably familiar with the catalogs of stars, giving right ascension, declination, distance from the sun, magnitude, spectral class, and so on. These catalogs are usually arranged in order of increasing right ascension. Thus, if you want to find all the GV-class stars, for example, you would have to search through the whole catalog. If you were interested only in those G-class stars within the constellation Scorpio, you would have another search to do. By using well-known methods of constructing files of records, each record being a particular star and each field being a specific

The inventory, or index,
of data files on a disk

datum about that star, you could create a star data file and then write a sorting program to find any particular kind of star you wished, for whatever purpose you have in mind.

Such files can be a help in chemistry, too, or in almost any area where you must sort large amounts of information. If you are interested in the problems of data file creation and management, perhaps you can explain and demonstrate how such files, records, and fields are defined, and why they are defined. Can you also show how a program accepts user input to the file?

One of the most common things done to a file is to sort it. Using any sorting algorithm, such as a bubble sort, write a program that shows, on the screen, each step as it occurs. Explain how the sort works. There are other sorting algorithms that are faster. Can you explain how these work?

There are three basic kinds of files—sequential, random, and indexed. What is the difference between them? Each has different limitations, strengths, and weaknesses. Can you explain these, and their relative ease or difficulty of use? How is one better for some applications and another better for a different task? Your display should not just use these files but demonstrate and explain, in the program itself if possible, what they are and why that particular form was chosen.

Although business is by no means a science, there are mathematical principles and computer science concepts that govern some of the problems businesses must solve. Besides data processing, computers in business are being used more and more frequently for office management, in areas such as interoffice communication, accounting, inventory control, and word processing.

Any one of these or other data operations is quite simple and can easily be handled by a person. It's when there are hundreds of checks to write, thousands of samples to measure, or millions of names to sort that the use of the computer becomes necessary.

A WRITER'S TOOL

One of the most common ways in which businesses are being automated is in the area of word processing. (This book is being composed, written, and revised on a word processor.) It goes almost without saying that if your project entails the writing of a report, a word processor can be of help to you.

But have you ever thought about what it takes to write a word processing program? A number of articles have appeared in computer magazines on how to develop a simple text editing program, even using a language such as BASIC. The more sophisticated word processors, written in assembly language, or sometimes in Pascal or C, have dozens of special features, so many that it is hard to choose which one is right for you. Can you write a simple word processing program, using any language you know? Make it as user-friendly as possible. Perhaps you can diagram or demonstrate some of the "tricks" word processors use, such as word wrap, insert, search and replace, and so on. Why are some features essential and others just fancy extras? What special features would you most like to have in a word processor, and can you write at least a partial program that would include those features?

Computers can manipulate parts of strings, as well as fields within a record. They can count the frequency of words within a sentence or paragraph, or a whole file of text. They can plug words into blanks left by the writer, according to rules or purely at random. Computer programs that "write" poetry frequently use a plug-in method, that is, a poetic structure is defined, and the places of various nouns, verbs, adverbs, and pronouns are left blank, to be filled randomly from a set of lists. Write a program that will "create" free verse or sonnets or a poem in the style of your favorite poet.

For creating computer prose, a good understanding of the grammatical structures that underlie our language is necessary. When words combine to form sentences, they follow certain rules. Various parts of speech are used in different ways. Can you write a program that will produce a grammatically correct sentence from just a list of words?

ARTIFICIAL LANGUAGE

One of the things some students of language have tried to do is understand the nature of language itself—not speech, but the grammar, syntax, word structure, and so on. One particularly interesting study involves the frequency of letters in a written text. Cryptanalysis has shown that certain letters occur more frequently than others in our language. When a program was written to make up "words" using these letters randomly, the results were gibberish. Subsequent studies looked at how letters were paired. What is the most frequent letter to follow A, B, C, and so on? Which letters begin most words, or end most words? Applying the frequency of letter pairs produced "words" that looked a bit more like English. When groups of three letters were used, the words were even more Englishlike. These frequencies are different for different languages, of course, and when a French text was analyzed, the "words" that were created came out looking like French.

You can write a program of your own to do this. Part of the problem here is providing the computer with enough text to sample, and providing it in such a way that the computer can count the letters and pairs, or triples, beginning and ending letters, and so on. For this you will almost certainly need a data file instead of statements embedded within the program. The sample text should be on the order of at least a thousand words long, and ten thousand would be better.

Also, what should the text be? If you merely copy words from a dictionary, you will get a "dictionary" as a result. That is, in a dictionary, each word occurs only once.

But in prose, many words are repeated. In this chapter, the word "the" occurs seventy-five times, "computer" occurs eleven times, and the word "Scorpio" occurs only once before this paragraph. Word frequency in newspapers is different from what it is in fine literature or poetry, so the sample text you use will have an effect on the kinds and frequency of words produced by your program.

This takes us a long way from what is commonly understood as data processing, but it is still the manipulation of information, which is something a computer does quite well.

3
NUMERICAL CALCULATION

It used to be that the only thing a computer did was work on hideously complex formulas, such as those used in long-range ballistics, or do simple calculations thousands of times. And that is still what computers are best known for. But we know that computers can do much more than that, and with the advent of programmable calculators, computers are called on less and less these days for the simpler kinds of problem-solving. Still, there are some calculation problems that take many hours to solve even on the fastest computers. Today, most home computers are being used almost exclusively to produce graphics, play games with, or run prepackaged software. We tend to forget the powerful mathematical capabilities of even the cheapest machine.

Any project that requires extensive mathematical calculation can benefit from using a computer, even if it is used only to do the arithmetic. Indeed, the need for extensive, repetitious, or complex calculation is one of the best reasons to use your computer in your project. This may require that you write a special program in order to solve your problem or analyze your data, but that program can be an impressive addition to your work.

A simple program—or even a complex one—that merely solves the problem would not add much to a display, however, even if it provided you with answers. Your project could be improved significantly by a computer display of the mathematical procedures involved. Using the computer's formatting capabilities, you should make every effort to have the display or printout be as clear and as well designed as possible.

If the mathematics involved required special algorithms (step-by-step procedures), these should be shown and displayed, and explained if necessary, so that people can see how they were used to manipulate the data. If, in the course of creating these algorithms, you went through any significant intermediate steps, these could also be shown, to illustrate how you achieved the final solution.

To further enhance your numerical display, you could show, by means of posters, how the data was changed from raw numbers into a graph or diagram. Many people do not understand how graphs work, or the proper way to display them, and an explanation of this will improve the professionalism of your project.

ROUTINES AND SUBROUTINES

It is true that today's pocket calculators, with their built-in functions, can solve almost all of our one-shot mathematical problems, and much of our more complicated calculating as well. Programmable calculators, with their ability to combine built-in functions in various ways, can handle quite sophisticated and complex computations. But if you want to perform the same operation a large number of times, use a large number of variables, work with a large amount of data, or have a printout of both the data and the results of the calculation, a computer is the best tool to use.

Without a computer or a calculator, in order to solve certain mathematical problems you would have to use a slide rule, a table of logarithms, trigonometric and other functions, and so on, or depend on your own mental pro-

Today's "pocket" computers, which look more like calculators, are powerful tools for solving difficult mathematical problems. The difference between calculators and computers is the computer's ability to be programmed, though most modern calculators have some limited memory capabilities.

cesses. Such work, if extensive, can be quite tedious and prone to error. If your project will involve either repetitious or complicated computation, you would be better off writing a program or using an already existing algorithm.

There are a number of books available that contain scientific subroutines and algorithms and that give some guidance on how to make the best use of them. These subroutines can sometimes be run by themselves, or they can be incorporated into a larger program. Most of these books assume that the programming language used will be BASIC, that being the one that comes with most popular home computers, and many of the programs are written with one type of computer in mind, such as the Apple or TRS-80. You might find you have to translate the program into your computer's version of BASIC. Other books, such as those used in college courses, might assume a knowledge of assembler language or another language, such as FORTRAN or PL/I. Using such a book could involve even more extensive translation problems.

If published routines exist that are just right for you, there is no reason for you not to use them. There will be many cases, however, where your problem will be quite special. Since your project idea will be original, no author can anticipate your needs. Therefore, you should be prepared to use a book of published routines primarily as a guide rather than as a sure solution to your specific problem.

A STELLAR MODEL

One case where a computer shines (pun intended) in doing calculations is in the design and construction of a model of the stars within the neighborhood of our sun. The computer makes use of its built-in trigonometric functions, of a stored program, of the ability to print out the results, and especially of stored data, which can be manipulated several times without having to type it in again.

There are thirty-seven star systems, made up of about fifty or fifty-five stars, within 5 parsecs of Sol. (One parsec, or second of parallax, equals about 3.26 light-years.) The uncertainty is due to the fact that some stars are assumed to be members of multiple-star systems, where an invisible body exerts a perturbation on the visible star's motion. Whether these bodies are giant planets, small stars, or the remnants of dead stars cannot easily be deduced.

Within 10 parsecs, there are over 190 star systems, and maybe more. Some stars are too small to be seen with the naked eye, and if far enough away, might not be seen even with a modern telescope, unless we happened to be looking in exactly the right place. And then, unless extensive observations are made, it is not easy to tell whether we are looking at a small star near us or a brighter star farther away. For that reason, we can only guess at the true number of stars within 10 parsecs.

Astronomy texts and other astronomy reference books give the physical data, where known, for these stars, including their distance and position relative to Sol. Sometimes distance is given as parallax, rather than as light-years or parsecs. All data given, usually in the form of tables, assumes Sol to be the center of the coordinate system, which is perfectly reasonable since that is our point of view. But this perspective, and the use of tables and even maps, makes it hard to visualize just how the various stars relate to each other. Exactly where is Alpha Centauri in relation to Betelgeuse or Epsilon Eridani?

To make these relationships clear, planetariums sometimes build a three-dimensional model, with each star a bead or ball, colored to represent its spectral class, suspended from a thread or fine wire. You can construct a similar model, drawing from astronomical references for your data.

For each star, you will have to convert the typical right ascension and declination figures to some other coordinate system, either cylindrical or Cartesian, whichever you are most comfortable with. This is so you will know from what point on your supporting board you will hang the star's string and how long that string will be. It requires a little trigonometry, and by using tables of trigonometric functions and a calculator, a single such computation would be quite easy.

But doing that same computation by hand thirty-seven times would be more than just tedious. With each repetition, the chance of reading the wrong line in the table, applying the wrong function, or misreading the results increases. A simple computer program to perform the same operation can be written within a short period of time and will never get tired or make errors. And if you decide to make a larger model, of the 190-plus stars within 10 parsecs of Sol, the saved effort becomes quite significant.

Of course, you will also have to load the data to be converted into the computer, either in the form of data statements in the program or as a data file. Errors can be made here, and the data, once entered, should be proofread and double-checked. The data can also be entered in response to program prompts, and if this method is used, error-trapping is very important.

NUMBER BASES

As a special kind of mathematical project, consider the arithmetic actually used by a computer. Computers store information in the form of binary numbers. Also, unless the computer has a special mathematical chip, all arithmetic is done as a series of additions. Even subtraction is done by adding, in this case, a negative number. This is sometimes hard for people to understand, and there are two ideas here.

The first idea is to illustrate arithmetic in bases other than 10. Since the computer uses binary numbers, can you write a program that, when run by someone who selects the decimal numbers and mathematical operations, demonstrates binary arithmetic? Can you show how that person's decimal numbers are converted into binary numbers? It is possible, using certain procedures, to convert a number in any base to any other, such as from base 8 to base 12, or base 17 to base 5. Can you show how this is done?

Some calculators, especially those intended for computer programmers, will convert decimal numbers to or from hexadecimal (base 16), and sometimes also octal (base 8). Can you explain why, though computer numbers are binary, programmers sometimes use these other number bases?

COMPUTER ARITHMETIC

The second idea involves the fact that even the most complex of arithmetic operations can be performed as a series of additions. If you wish to demonstrate how this is done, you should probably do it in base 10, to avoid confusing the observer. Again, the observer should be able to select the operations and the values to be worked upon. Performing multiplication, or even division, in this way is relatively easy, but can you take a square root using only addition? The binary arithmetic can be shown alongside the decimal arithmetic, if you wish.

Another special project might be to demonstrate how computers, which internally use only integer numbers within a certain range (the computer's precision), can sometimes also do double-precision calculations. Some computers use intermediate double-precision values when calculating a large number. Can you write a program to double even that? Can you demonstrate how it is done? How does a computer calculate scientific notation?

While discussing astronomical models, we mentioned converting from the given coordinate system to a cylindrical or Cartesian coordinate system. There can be other reasons for performing similar conversions, such as when preparing a map of the South Pole, or studying the way fruit drops from a tree. Each of these coordinate systems was developed with a particular use in mind. Can you provide an example of spherical, cylindrical, Cartesian, and polar coordinate systems and their primary uses? Can you think of any others, and explain how and why they are used? How do these relate to each other, and if a conversion is desired, how would that be done? How about a coordinate system that has time as an additional dimension?

4

DATA AND ITS ANALYSIS

Any study of the real world frequently produces massive amounts of information. In many experiments in zoology and botany, such as a study of the effects of nutrition on growth or the effects of deprivation or toxicity, thousands of sample cases may be tested. The results are often subtle and do not readily reveal their significance. Extraneous factors intrude, and scientists have developed the concepts of blind and double-blind testing to try to allow for this.

ANALOG INFORMATION

Sometimes the data to be analyzed will be in analog, instead of digital, form. This is when the data is from sensors of one kind or another, such as a joystick, voltmeter, or other device that uniformly measures electric current or potential.

The difference between analog and digital data is not always clearly understood, but it can be demonstrated. As an example, think of an elevator. There are two ways you can think about its position. If you ask how high up it is from the basement, and measure with a ruler, you will be measuring its analog position. That is, the length the ruler measures—47 feet, 6⅞ inches (approximately 14.5 m)—is an analog of how high up the elevator really is. If you tell what floor it's on, you are giving its digital position. It is either on the third floor or the fourth. It may be halfway in between, but there is no floor numbered 3½. Its height varies continuously and can never be measured precisely, while its floor number is discrete, one or another, even if you have to "watch your step."

The original computer was digital—the fingers. An abacus is also digital, in that discrete beads are in discrete positions. A slide rule, on the other hand, is analog. The slide moves continuously, each pair of scales representing various arithmetic operations, with the position of the slide giving an approximation of the value sought.

Electronic analog computers have been constructed and are still used extensively in certain areas, but digital computers are far more common. Can you explain how an analog computer works, and why, under certain circumstances, it might be preferable? Can you explain why digital computers now predominate?

No matter what project you have in mind, it may produce quite a bit of data. This data, as raw numbers, is of little help in determining what the experiment proved or didn't prove. It must be analyzed and studied, in a number of different ways. Just as we can use a computer to perform arithmetic operations, so we can use these operations to help us in our analyses.

INTO THE EARTH

The scientists who study the structure of the earth's mantle and core, and earthquakes, tectonics, and vulcanism, must depend in large part on the analysis of data. We can see volcanoes and feel when a fault slips, but the inner structure of the earth is hidden from us.

One of the ways we know about the core of our planet is that the waves produced by earthquakes are of two different kinds—transverse waves, which travel only through solids, and compression waves, which travel through both solids and fluids. When an earthquake occurs, seismometers at a number of locations record the intensity, type, duration, and frequency of each tremor. By analyzing this data, seismologists can get an idea of the depth of the crust and the thickness of the mantle. Carefully prepared explosions set off in the ground also cause vibrations, which can be analyzed to locate caves, oil deposits, or other discontinuities or formations. By comparing the waves received in new locations with those that have traveled through known structures, the scientist can predict with surprising accuracy what will be found if a mine shaft or core is sunk in that place.

If you can build a small seismometer, you can perform some experiments of your own. For example, if your device can detect the passage of a truck over a highway, can you tell the difference between a highway built on a rocky bed and one built on sand or gravel? You may have to make a number of trials, testing known ground first and then unknown stretches of highway. Or, from the strength of the vibrations, can you estimate the weight of the truck, or distinguish when two trucks pass over at the same time instead of a single, heavier vehicle? Are the vibrations produced in a steel bridge different from those in a concrete bridge? It might be possible to tell, by the form and strength and route of vibrations in a bridge, whether it is sound or has invisible flaws that should be repaired.

The floors in most buildings are not quite as solid as they seem. Many people have had the experience of not walking softly enough near a stereo and hearing the needle bounce on the record. Can you determine the structure of the supports under the floor just by examining the vibrations made when someone jumps up and down at various locations in the room? Such vibrations might indicate that a heavy object, such as a refrigerator or waterbed, might need extra support under the floor to keep it from buckling or sagging.

Computer graphics could be used to show the underlying structures you have discovered from an analysis of your data, even if that data does not require computer time itself. Seismologists, of course, have years worth of data with which they hope to be able to predict earthquakes, or at least learn where they are most likely to occur, so that proper precautions can be taken, such as reinforcing buildings and other structures. Computer programs designed to answer questions like these might be beyond your scope, but you can apply the same principles to situations easier to understand, to illustrate how problems like these are handled.

THE LAWS OF CHANCE

Elementary statistics is probably the most common form of data analysis. We use it to answer such questions as: What is the mean or average of a sequence of numbers? How much does a number vary from an expected value? What is the chance of a particular value occurring? Is an occurrence chance, or does it mean something important is happening?

Both statistics and the related study of probability are difficult to master, but their elementary principles are used in the analysis of most data, and some of these principles we use, more or less automatically, all the time. For example, can you show, graphically, the difference between the mean, the median, and the mode of a set of data? Sometimes averages must be weighed to counterbalance conditions that might lead to an incorrect interpretation. Can you show how and why this is done?

When you collect a set of data, there is a range over which the data is distributed. It is frequently necessary to know how much a particular measurement varies from a mean. This is called the mean deviation. How does the standard deviation differ, and why is it used? If your data involves the measure of only one variable, such as height or age, your analysis is much simpler than if it involves two or more variables, such as both height and weight. This is multivariate data. What kind of special considerations must be taken into account in this case?

Probability is even harder for some people to understand and accept, but is an important part of most statistical analyses. It involves the theory of random numbers, some ideas of set theory, and the notion of independence versus dependence. When applied to statistics, probability allows inference and hypothesis testing. Can you demonstrate concepts of probability using dice or a deck of cards? How are they used for estimation and testing?

Many pocket calculators have basic statistical functions built in, but the calculator's memory is not big enough to store the large amounts of data typically used in any statistical examination. If only a few data items are to be considered, and only one or two functions are to be applied, this data can be entered by hand quite easily. But if there are hundreds or thousands of items and a series of statistical tests to be performed, even a programmable calculator would have difficulty—if it could do the work at all—especially if the subsequent tests are dependent on the results of earlier tests. If a complex or specialized statistical procedure is to be performed, or if there are a number of sets of data, all of which are to be tested in the same way, then a computer program is invaluable, and may provide the only way for the work to be done.

TELLING IT TO THE COMPUTER

If you have relatively small amounts of data to be analyzed or otherwise used, user interaction is probably the easiest way of entering it into your computer program. Providing this interaction may be as simple as a prompt to hit the RETURN key for the next part of the program, or as complex as a data file management system. To be effective, the prompts that elicit information from the user must be clear, and the program must not accept a wrong response.

It does no good to have a program that waits for the user to hit a key to continue if there is no prompt to do so or if there are no instructions for which key to push. And if string data is requested, the program must not accept numerical data, store false data, or crash. Instead it should be able to ask again for the right information. This is especially true if the data is to be provided by someone other than yourself, and is of the utmost importance in the creation of a data file. Also, what happens if the data you enter has more characters than the program allows? How can you provide for this, so that the program detects an overly long entry and asks for a retry?

Can you explain how a computer can wait for user input, and how it can test for proper input and not crash when the wrong kind of entry is made? Can you demonstrate how a program can run itself, going back to the beginning when it has finished? Don't just have the program do this; show how it is done. If you can do that with the program itself, it will be more impressive, but you could instead use supplementary materials, such as posters of flowcharts, showing just what happens whenever the program pauses and the observer responds to the prompt.

Once data is loaded, any number of operations can be performed upon it, without having to enter the data again. Thus, if you are performing statistical tests and the first one is uninformative, you can try another. Too many failures might indicate that in fact there is no significance to your data, which in itself is worth knowing.

POLLING THE PEOPLE

One source of data for statistical analysis, and an important tool of business and political researchers, is the demographic study. The population is polled to determine such things as average income level, distribution of ethnic groups, concentrations of high or low educational levels, preferences in automobile tires, frequency of specific medical complaints, and on and on.

The decennial census is one of the broadest of demographic studies, but smaller studies are conducted with more depth. A poll in *Omni* or *Reader's Digest* is a kind of demographic study, where opinions are solicited and matched with other characteristics, such as age, education, or sex. Almost any area of human activity can be analyzed in this way. If the results are simply reported, that is, people or things or activities are merely tallied, the study is considered descriptive statistics. When inferences or conclusions are drawn from those results, and the census-taker seeks to eliminate the effects of chance and predict the future, it is called analytical statistics.

You can do a demographic survey of your own, but there are special sampling techniques you should use to ensure the validity of your data. You have to define your population—the people on your block or in your town or crossing Main Street from noon to 1:00 p.m.—and then query only a certain number of those, a representative sample, according to one of three sets of criteria: (1) the sample is random; (2) it is systematic, such as every tenth person; or (3) it is stratified, that is, if your population is half men and half women, then the sample, either random or systematic, is also half men and half women.

If you poll just your neighborhood, and only between the hours of 7:00 p.m. and 9:00 p.m., will you get the same information as if you went around between nine and eleven in the morning? If you're interested only in homemakers and people who work at home, you might, but if you're interested in the population as a whole, including those who work during the day or go to school, you will miss many of them if you ask at the wrong time of day. If you knock on a door and nobody is home or they won't answer, can you just ignore them? Can you ask someone else next door instead? Should you record them as not available, a kind of special nonanswer? Sociologists and others who make it their business to find out what people are thinking have gone to considerable effort to make sure that their sampling methods truly reflect the population being polled. What is the right thing to do?

Your subject need not be complex or profound, but your questions should include some that will provide background information. It is not enough to just ask people, for example, whether they own a home computer. You should also try to find out what their income is, what kind of job they hold, how many children they have and what ages they are, and what previous experience they might have had with large computers. It is this information, combined with the results of your special questions, which provides meaningful information about computer use.

5

COMPUTER GRAPHICS

The ability to produce graphics, pictorial images of one sort or another, is one of the computer's most useful and interesting functions. You should certainly make extensive use of graphics, if your computer has the capability, in almost any project you do. And, as an area of computer science, graphics can be a good source of projects itself.

Mostly we take the computer screen for granted, paying attention only to what is displayed on it. Very little thought is given to how the image is produced. Although very much like a TV, a video screen does not produce a picture in quite the same way. The characters and graphics symbols, for example, are formed in a dot matrix. And although these dots may look coarse compared to a TV picture, it actually requires greater resolution than a TV can provide to display a line of eighty characters. Can you explain why this is so? A magnifying glass could be used to make these dots clearer.

MAKING A PICTURE

Not all microcomputers have graphics capabilities, but most of the popular home computers do. These are usually made use of by program commands, most frequently in BASIC, the "native" language of most home computers. Some versions of BASIC do not have special graphics commands, such as **DRAW** or **LINE**, and have to rely on **PEEK,** which looks at an address in memory, and **POKE,** which puts a value directly into an address. Although using **PEEK** and **POKE** is tedious, and these commands are usually used for other purposes, they can be incorporated into BASIC statements to give some graphics abilities.

LOGO also has special graphics commands, but they differ considerably from BASIC commands, in form if not in function. How can you demonstrate the differences between BASIC and LOGO graphics, as far as the user is concerned?

Even low-resolution block graphics can be explored. Can you write a program that will let users put a graphic shape wherever they want it, to let them build pictures of their own? This involves some knowledge of screen memory and formatting techniques. Your program should let the user employ understandable X and Y coordinates rather than **POKE** statements. To make this even clearer, the screen could have a border with numbers on the X and Y axes—on both sides and top and bottom—so that the user can see just where the shape is going to go. This might restrict the overall area available to the user, however. If he or she tries to put a shape somewhere beyond the borders, what will happen?

Alternatively, a picture-drawing program could make use of a cursor controlled by a joystick or cursor keys. When the cursor is in the right place, a shape key could be hit to print the shape right there. This would be especially useful on computers that have graphic block shapes printed on the keyboard.

Images can move, sometimes by scrolling, sometimes by page flipping, and sometimes by redrawing all or part of the picture. This will depend a great deal on the kind of computer you are using. Sprites and player/missiles are yet another machine-dependent form of animation. Depending on what your computer can do, can you explain, by using the graphics themselves, how this animation is accomplished? You might want to use supplementary materials, such as flowcharts, screen diagrams, or a chart of screen memory to help you out.

THE ARTIST'S LANGUAGE

When you use a BASIC graphics command, it actually does several things. For example, if you have defined certain areas on the screen, the command **PAINT 7, 250, 175** will test to find the border of the area that contains the point X=250, Y=175, and then will fill it with the color desired, in this case color number 7. What is the logical structure of this command, or of others such as **CIRCLE, POINT, DRAW?**

There are special graphics languages that make the whole process of producing pictures and other forms of graphics much easier. Some of these make use of a light pen or a cursor, instead of X and Y coordinates. Others simply combine elementary commands in complex ways, so that you can do a lot with just a few words. What is their logical structure? Can you write a simple graphics language in BASIC or assembly? If you know FORTH, this should be easy. How would such a special language be better than the more typical BASIC type of graphics commands?

Graphics languages and special graphics commands are preferred because you can do more complicated things with a single instruction, or with a series of instructions that are clearly understood. **POKE 35768,52** doesn't tell you much about what the effect will be, but **PRINT 'A' AT X=25, Y=10** does. If you are a computer artist, what special features would you like your graphics language to have? Why? If you are familiar with FORTH, explain how such a graphics language could be built up from primitives.

THE UNARTISTIC SCREEN

Even computers or terminals that do not have graphics have special commands, frequently escape codes, that can put alphanumerics anywhere on the screen, for example, by first locating the cursor with an X-Y coordinate and then printing the character. These escape codes, on some terminals, can also make the characters half intensity, inverse video, or underlined. Sometimes a character or word can be made invisible, or certain areas of the screen can be protected so that the cursor won't go there. Most people never have the occasion to use commands such as these, and they are not always easy to use. Can you write a program that makes use of these screen-formatting commands? It should let people put characters wherever they wish and should also explain how the commands work and how the screen works.

    The computer not only can put a character anywhere, it can also scan its screen memory and find out what already is at a particular place. It "reads" the screen. Compare screen memory to the actual screen, and explain how the computer does this. Can you write a program that graphically demonstrates just what is going on when a character is so placed or read? Good error-trapping and prompting will be necessary if the program is to be interactive and not just automatic.

THE MATHEMATICS OF ART

Any graphics you produce to illustrate your project should have an artistic element to it; good artistic design of your computer displays will enhance their attractiveness and professional "feel." Computer art itself is something special. As art, it can be displayed on a screen, outputted on a printer, or reproduced with a plotter.

    The earliest form of computer art was the graphic representation of mathematical functions. Variables were assigned a range of values and frequently displayed to resemble a convoluted surface composed of lines or dots. The problem of "hidden lines," that is, those parts of a picture that are "behind" other parts and therefore should not be seen, has to be solved, of course. The orientation of the resulting image can be changed, and the axes drawn to different scales to emphasize or deemphasize certain features.

Some mathematical functions in which you might have no particular interest could be explored, simply for the nature of the shapes they produce. Abstract patterns can be produced in a similar way, by varying a pattern for successive passes of the pen or cursor. If you can print out these patterns on a printer or plotter, they could supplement your screen display. You might also include an explanation of the functions or mathematical principles used to produce the patterns.

A special kind of computer art is known as turtle graphics. Originally created as a part of the LOGO computer language, there are now other software packages that can produce turtle graphics. One can move the turtle around on the screen by direct commands or, by means of a program, produce rather complex geometric designs. The mathematics behind some of these designs is rather intricate. You can use turtle graphics to explain a number of geometric principles, some of them rather sophisticated. On the other hand, you can use your knowledge of geometry to explain how some of the more complicated pictures were created.

You can also think of the turtle as a kind of robot. In this case, the picture produced is not as important as the program that tells the turtle where to go. If the turtle moves by keyboard commands, can you explain what those commands mean and how they are interpreted by the computer? Such an explanation would probably be best if embedded within an interactive demonstration program. If the turtle moves by using a joystick, can you show how that works?

A REMINDER

Materials due on the last date stamped below. Overdue fine 10¢ per day.

NOTE: Any item deposited in the book drop within 1 hour of closing will be recorded on the following working day's transactions.

SEP 09 1989

OCT 2 8 1989

DEC 1 9 1989

SALT LAKE COUNTY LIBRARY SYSTEM
For Information, Call 943-4636

C 16A-489

Using turtle graphics is so easy that even small children can master it in a short time. And although some of the more complex patterns require rather sophisticated algorithms, here is another place where you could write an interactive program, to let the observer create elaborate pictures without having to go through the programming process. This might be in the form of a menu, allowing the user to select the amount of movement, the degree of turn, the number of repetitions—pen up or pen down—and so on. This could be strictly interactive, with each selection being performed immediately or, at the user's option, the program could wait until a whole series of commands was given, which would then be performed all at once, at the end of the series.

PIXELS AND PATTERNS

In some shopping malls, you can find people who will take your picture with a TV camera and reproduce the image with a printer on paper or a tee shirt. If you or your school has access to equipment like this, here is an opportunity to explore the principles of TV imaging, digitizing, and the ability of people to recognize a picture when its detail has been reduced. How is the image from the TV camera converted into picture elements, or pixels? How are light values assigned? How are these values converted into a printed image?

Computer art has practical applications as well, beyond those suggested so far. The designing of quilts, needlepoint, and weaving frequently requires that the artist draw out the pattern and then modify and often redraw it, sometimes many times. Computer programs can produce these patterns on the screen and perhaps reproduce them on paper later. Such programs would allow the artist to make a small change at the keyboard and see the results instantly.

Many of these patterns make use of repetition, and

Computer graphics are a vital part of manufacturing and engineering activities today.

your program could allow the artist to draw, on the screen, the basic element only, then perform the repetitions all at once. Here is a place where symmetry is important. A pattern, sometimes a triangle with unequal sides or sometimes the letter R, is used to show forms of symmetry. For example, the R can be glided, that is, repeated side by side. It can be rotated so that it stands on its head. Or the R can be reflected, as in a mirror. There are other forms of symmetry, and they can be combined in various ways. Can you reproduce these or other operations, as they are called, on a graphic image? Can you add an element to the middle or edge of a basic pattern, and then have the computer redraw the whole? Border patterns have to turn corners, a special kind of mirroring. A duplicated pattern might alternate colors from one repeat to another. Can you use the computer to duplicate some of the complicated tilings of M. C. Escher?

Here is another area where an interactive program would be fascinating, allowing the observer to make any change he or she desired to an existing pattern, or to create a new one from a few simple elements. Menus and special error-trapping techniques might be helpful. You could supplement this with printouts demonstrating artistic design principles.

Of course, if you are an accomplished computer artist, you can just show off your talents. Computer animation is heavily used in commercial graphics (see almost any television ad). It is also used in training programs for air pilots and sea captains, and for computer-aided design and engineering. This is an area of computer science which can provide both challenges and opportunities for the aspiring student. What you produce for a science fair should, of course, emphasize the computer science aspect of your graphics, and any such razzle-dazzle display should also incorporate, in the program or with supplementary materials, an explanation or demonstration of the graphics principles involved.

6

PICTORIAL REPRESENTATION

The first thing anybody notices when they come up to a computer is its screen. You can take advantage of this to produce a pictorial display, which is sometimes the best way to present the results of your project. A computer display is good showmanship, even if the project did not require computation or computer analysis of data, and it gives you a chance to demonstrate your skills in computer graphics.

Moving images on a computer screen can be more attractive and look more professional than posters. Also, the use of graphics, even more than movies perhaps, can demonstrate how something changes over time. This is especially valuable when the time for the actual process is either very long, say years, decades, or millennia, or very short, as a few seconds or even a fraction of a second. By use of computer graphics, we can greatly compress or expand the time scale.

LIFE OF A STAR

We think we know how a star evolves because countless observations have been made, and because mathematical models have been constructed that seek to describe the process and predict what would happen if conditions were different. Evolutionary tracks of stars are frequently drawn on HR diagrams, which compare a star's brightness with its color and temperature.

In fact, no one has ever seen a star change from main sequence to red giant to nova to white dwarf. The time scale is too large. But given our knowledge of physics, the effects of mass, gravity, and temperature (all interrelated), and the chemical composition of a star, we can make some pretty good guesses as to how a star evolves from a given beginning.

You can demonstrate your knowledge of these principles quite graphically on a computer screen. Starting with a star of any given mass, you can show by a sequence of pictures how long it takes before the protostar actually forms, how long it will stay on the main sequence, and, when it finally grows old, what its path across the rest of the diagram will be. Your time scale might be a million years a second or even greater, in order to get the whole life cycle of a star into a minute or two of demonstration.

THE ACTIVE EARTH

The movement of the continents, according to the theory of plate tectonics, took place over many millions of years. A study of the shapes of today's landmasses seems to indicate that they once all fitted together to form a single, giant continent called Pangaea. As interesting as this idea is, a display consisting of drawings taken from books and magazines might seem rather unoriginal. Also, there are usually only three or four maps given in any discussion of continental drift, each one many millions of years apart from the next.

If your computer has color graphics, however, you could re-create these simplified maps and then show the landmasses in intermediate stages as the continents changed from Pangaea to those of today. If you can't fit the whole world onto your screen, you could concentrate on just one of the more spectacular events, such as India drifting up and colliding with the Asian continent to create the Himalayan mountains.

But these are still static pictures. What if you had a "clock" in the upper right corner of the screen, counting down the years, and could show, by successive pages or whatever graphics tricks you know, the continents actually moving? Your display would be impressive.

Some experts try to predict where the continents will be in the future. What might our planet look like in a million years, or a billion years? A few years back a lot of people were worried that California might slip into the ocean. Will tectonic forces along the San Andreas fault make California slide around the Pacific basin and end up near Japan? Continents do move, though usually with little overall effect on global conditions. But if Antarctica shifted from its polar position, thus releasing the water held as ice into the oceans, how would the resulting increase in sea level of a few inches, or a hundred feet, affect coastlines?

Another aspect of plate tectonics is vulcanism. Volcanoes can be simulated with sand and air or water, but computer graphics can show some of the same processes. When the ocean floor spreads, as it does in the mid-Atlantic, it releases molten material from below. In other places, one plate slides under another, and the release of molten rock to the surface here is somewhat different. In still other places, where the plates slide back and forth, explosively violent volcanoes are the result. Mount St. Helens in Washington and El Chichón in Mexico are examples.

Each of these forms of vulcanism is slightly different from the others. Can you explain the differences? Using computer graphics, in a cross-section image, show how the magma below the crust moves up and escapes onto the surface.

Volcanoes are simply piles of once-molten rock. The mountains formed by the collision of crustal plates are much larger, and in some ways more spectacular. The processes that form these mountains are so slow that even cold stone bends instead of breaking, like layered sheets of plasticene instead of dried clay. They are folded, arched, twisted, and sometimes even turned upside down.

We can get only a hint of this by examining what is left of older mountains. For as powerful as the forces of vulcanism and crustal movement are, the effects of weather and erosion are equally strong. The gentle rain that falls to earth and the spring breezes cut away the stone and wear it down, changing the very shape of the earth itself.

Here is another area where cross-section graphics can be quite useful; they can show just how a folded mountain was formed and then eroded, for example, to produce the familiar Appalachians or Rockies of today. On an even smaller scale, the structures known as geosynclines can be graphically illustrated on the computer.

Rivers that cut through rock and sediment reveal the layers underneath. The courses of rivers themselves are influenced by the shape of the land and the nature of the rock over which they flow. The Mississippi River, and the Colorado where it flows through the Grand Canyon, are very different. The Mississippi did not create the broad plains that surround it, but the Grand Canyon is a direct result of the Colorado's erosion. Can you show what the land looked like before the rivers did their work? How about the grinding effects of glaciers, which polish land flat but leave terminal moraines?

THE SOLID MINERALS

Vulcanism not only makes mountains, it also helps in the formation of a number of familiar minerals. Many of these minerals take the form of crystals, and the study of crystals is an important part of geology and other scientific disciplines.

Crystals are fascinating. We wear them as jewelry and use them to decorate our homes. Crystals are orderly arrangements of atoms, which in themselves cannot be seen. Computer pictures can be used to show the various ways in which the atoms of a crystal are organized. How many such ways are there? Which are most common and which least common? How do the arrangements, and the bonds between atoms, determine the faces of crystals or their lines of cleavage? Can you show the difference between graphite and diamond? This may require that you learn some of the methods of 3-D graphics.

An important aspect of crystallography is symmetry. There are seventeen forms of symmetry in two dimensions and many, many more in three dimensions (though most of these seldom appear in crystals). The principles of two-dimensional symmetry can be illustrated even with block graphics. Three-dimensional symmetry is probably beyond what most small computers can do, and when you add color to the study, the forms become very complex indeed.

Not all arrangements of atoms are symmetrical. The study of chemistry in large part deals with nonsymmetrical arrangements. Each atom can bond with other atoms only in certain ways, and the number and kind of connections determine the kinds of molecules and compounds that result. If your project is in chemistry, color graphics can enhance your diagrams of molecular structures.

MOLECULES IN MOTION

When molecules of a compound do not remain in fixed positions, what we have is a fluid—either a liquid or a gas. Fluid dynamics, which is the study of how molecules in a fluid interact with each other and their environment, helps

The properties of coal being
analyzed by a computer program.

describe how an airplane wing produces lift, how winds circulate around the globe, and how sound moves through the air. Again, computer pictures can help demonstrate some of these complex principles.

Acoustics, as a special kind of fluid dynamics, has its own laws and principles. Sound is a phenomenon of the air, moving from the source in a series of waves. One of the primary concerns of acoustical engineers is the way a theater reflects sound from the stage to the audience. The waves reflect in much the same way light does, though not exactly. Sound is reflected and absorbed. It is also bent by obstacles in its path.

There is a phenomenon known as a whispering gallery. The simplest form is an elliptical chamber with sound-reflecting walls. A person standing at one epicenter can whisper so softly that others only a few feet away cannot hear. Yet someone at the other epicenter can hear him or her perfectly. The movement of the sound can be illustrated graphically, and if the principles of absorption, reflection, and refraction are also understood, the acoustical properties of rooms or buildings of varying sizes and shapes can be simulated with computer pictures.

TRACES OF HUMANKIND

Another study of structures, one entirely different, is that of buildings and other artifacts left by vanished peoples or cultures. Archaeologists on a "dig" are careful to note just where each artifact is found in relation to the overall site and to other artifacts found nearby. Computer graphics could be used to present a visual display of a site and then allow the observer to, figuratively speaking, strip off layer after layer, to study the artifacts' positions and relationships at leisure.

It has been determined that Stonehenge was built in several stages. Sometimes old structures were removed before new ones were added. A graphic model of the post holes and monolith positions could be presented, to show how the structure changed over time.

Graphics could also be used to show the astronomical principles thought to be behind the design of Stonehenge and other such structures. Using a plan of the monument, show the position of the sun at the spring and fall equinoxes and other significant times, and show how the shadows of the rising sun were used to mark these special days.

Sometimes only a fragment of an artifact is found. Computer graphics can be used to help determine the most likely configuration of the whole. And, of course, statistics can be used to discover whether there is any meaning or significance to the number and position of stone tools found at a site, and whether they signify temporary dwellings, worksites, dumps, or just randomly scattered implements.

Prehistoric art changed and evolved over time and was influenced by outside cultural sources. Computer graphics can illustrate this evolution. Similar patterns can be compared, to help decide which came first, or which was local and which foreign.

COMPUTER "ART" IN SCIENCE . . .

What we have been doing so far is to use the ability of the computer to create visual images of states or processes, to help us better understand them. Scientists, too, use computer graphics. In fact, computer graphics today is one of science's most sophisticated research tools.

In medicine, for example, computer graphics is used extensively in acoustic imaging, microwave imaging, CAT scans, and so on, enabling us to see inside the body without actually cutting the skin and opening it up. Graphics are used in astronomy to show us what the sky might look like if we could "see" X rays or radio frequencies. Computer images help in the testing of industrial materials and processes. Far from being a pretty extra, computer graphics is becoming indispensible to basic research and industrial development.

Without access to very expensive equipment and software, you cannot duplicate uses such as these. But you can demonstrate your knowledge of how they work and what they mean—what they let the researcher or doctor know about the progress or treatment of the disease, the significance of "hot-spots" in the galaxy, or the changes in stress when a beam or building is subjected to extreme external forces.

. . . AND IN SOCIETY

Not all graphics demonstrations, however, need to be imitations of the methods used for computer imaging. Nor are such graphics used only in "hard" scientific research. As we learn more about the way people behave in and interact with their environment, we learn more about their special needs in certain situations. One area of that study is environmental design. This can include projects as grand as renovating a whole business district or as narrow as designing the layout of an office, and here, too, the computer and its ability to produce pictorial representations have their place.

The study of existing automobile traffic patterns helps the planner decide where to put a new highway or which road to widen. Graphics, of course, would be only a part of such a project. A study of physiology helps design more comfortable chairs, and determines the right height for kitchen counters and the tolerance of noise levels.

Traffic patterns in an office would also make for an interesting study. You will need to know who spends most of his or her time sitting at a desk and who frequently visits other people. How far apart should desks be to permit easy movement, and how close can they come together before people feel like they're sitting in each other's laps? Until recently, most studies of office design were done by moving paper cutouts around on a sheet of graph paper. Can you apply these principles to the layout of desks and computers in your classroom?

Room layouts are especially amenable to computer graphic modeling. Pictures can not only be drawn, they can be made to move, in whole or in part. If you have player/missile or sprite graphics, it could be especially useful for room design, where each item of furniture can be a sprite placed against the background of the walls and doors.

Such graphics could also be used to design the layout of factories, restaurants, or other establishments where actually moving the furniture, to find the best placement, can be tedious at best or, in the case of heavy machinery, next to impossible. From here you could easily move into perhaps more sophisticated problems of architecture, city design, and so on.

THOSE WITH SPECIAL PROBLEMS

Some people have special problems in getting along in our world. The handicapped frequently need extra help. Computers have already been used, for example, to provide a voice for those who can't speak. Some of the most innovative aids for the handicapped have been built from inexpensive computer components. What is needed is an understanding of the handicap and an idea of the kind of help needed. If you have a handicap of your own, or know someone who has, you can do a project that will have more than theoretical interest. Amateur solutions to handicap problems can be of real help to others.

A special kind of problem is an inability to read, either because of inadequate education, a mental handicap, or because the person is foreign (and is perhaps literate in another language). There has been some effort to design a set of universal symbols to be used in place of the written word. Modern highway signs make some use of this, as do certain signs in airports. Computerized systems of this

Many sign language programs have been developed to aid the deaf in learning to "speak."

sort could also assist cerebral palsy victims and others who cannot communicate in any of the usual ways.

In developing these now-familiar signs, dozens of symbols were created to represent the message to be communicated. These were then tested by showing them to people and asking them if they understood what the symbol meant. Can you create symbols to convey special messages, such as "Hit RETURN to continue"? Try several different symbols representing the same thing, and test them out on your class.

LIGHT AND COLOR

Even if you have little facility with graphics, computers can be used very effectively in some quite simple displays. One of these might be the study of light and color.

One characteristic of light is that it comes in different colors, or wavelengths. When we see a photograph or a painting, what we see are the wavelengths of light that are reflected from the surface. In the study of art in school we learn the principles of color mixing—red and yellow make orange, and so on. This is easy to demonstrate with watercolors.

When we watch television, on the other hand, we are seeing colors transmitted directly rather than reflected. This is rather more difficult to demonstrate. It can be done with colored films of the kind used in movie and TV studios. The film absorbs all colors but those it transmits; these colors can then be shown on white paper. Or, transmitted colors can be shown on the screen of a computer.

A close look at the spots of light on the TV screen or monitor shows that there are only three colors: red, blue, and green. Yet, when we mix red and green, what we see is yellow. If you are exploring the theories of transmitted color, your computer can be a great help in setting up a demonstration of how it works.

By means of color graphics, you can do more than just show patches of light mixing to form new colors. You can give shapes to the areas of color, change their size, and move them around the screen in an interesting fashion. If your computer can produce colors of varying intensities, or brightnesses, you can add even more detail to your demonstration.

THE ART OF MATHEMATICS

Graphics can be used to illustrate even intangible concepts, by means of diagrams. Formal logic, for example, is not always easy to understand. The solutions to logic problems such as are found in periodicals require a certain approach and certain procedures. Can you demonstrate this? The kind of logic used by computers is somewhat different. Can you explain the similarities and differences and display this graphically and interactively?

Aside from the graphs and charts that show quantitative data (the subject of the next chapter), computer pictures can help clarify mathematical concepts. Trigonometry, which involves the study of the sides and angles of a right triangle in relation to each other, is used in many areas of physics. Can you show how the ratios of a right triangle—sine, tangent, secant, cosine, cotangent, and cosecant—can be used to determine distances we cannot measure directly? Can you demonstrate how we know that these functions remain true, regardless of the size of the triangle?

Calculus involves the concepts of infinite sequences, the limits of those sequences, infinity, and infinitesimal measurements of the rate of a function change. The discipline is essential to the solution of many problems of mathematics, physics, and other sciences. Sometimes the best way to express the concepts involved is by means of pictures or graphs.

Conic sections can be displayed graphically, showing how a plane, cutting through the cone at various angles, produces circles, ellipses, parabolas, and hyperbolas. This can be done with two pictures. The first shows the double cone, point to point, from the side. The plane that cuts the cones is shown as a line. The second picture is the shape of the face that results as the plane is rotated across the cones. When the plane is parallel to the base of the cone, it is a circle. As the plane rotates, the second figure becomes an ellipse, and so on.

A second way to show this is to illustrate how the shape of the figure changes as the foci move apart. With one focus, you have a circle. With two, for any distance less than infinity, you have increasingly oblate ellipses. With the second focus at infinity, you have the parabola, and as the second focus "comes back from negative infinity," you have hyperbolas.

Some of the objects of topological study are impossible to build, such as a Kline bottle. A computer picture could help to make the concept clear. In other cases, topological identities are well understood by some people, but not others. One special case is that of the solid with a hole—a key, a donut, a coffee cup, a needle, all of which are topologically identical. Animated graphics could be used in this and similar cases to prove that identity. Then there are knots, loops of a theoretical cord that are defined as knotted if they cannot be untangled without the ends passing through loops. Knot theory has other applications besides pure mathematics. Again, computer graphics could demonstrate the distinctions between two tangles, one of which was knotted and the other, closely resembling the first, which was not.

The story problems used to teach algebra often confuse people. We've all seen pictures of boats moving first upstream, then down; ladders leaning against a wall; buckets of different sizes holding fluids; and so on. Although getting a computer to perform truly algebraic manipulations (rather than just solve for variables) is not yet perfected, these and other story problems could be illustrated by computer graphics and their solutions displayed. Once you get started, of course, all this is just the beginning.

7
GRAPHS AND CHARTS

Although most mathematical investigations do not lend themselves well to visual displays, producing reports and papers rather than hard, physical results, there are a number of areas where, with the aid of a computer and its graphics capabilities, you can create a demonstration to illustrate the work you've done. Also, when the results of your experiment are in the form of numerical data, as opposed to changed living matter or the creation of a mechanical thing, a graphic as opposed to a tabular display will convey the information more concisely and have more impact.

Tables of numbers are hard to understand, and the relationships between values are not easy to visualize. For example, compare a statistical normal, or "bell," curve with the table from which the curve was drawn. Also, compare the table of values derived from calculating the sines of angles with the curve produced when those values are graphed. The tables are necessary to provide the actual numbers, but the graphs let us see, at a glance, what the table *means*.

A computer is not only able to solve equations giving values to be plotted on a graph, it can plot the graph itself. In our discussion of computer art, we mentioned the use of mathematical functions to produce interesting convoluted surfaces. Can you demonstrate the relationship between the members of a family of functions by varying the values of the coefficients or parameters? Parametric equations are simultaneous equations with the added dimension of time. Can you replace a series of hand-drawn graphs with a computer image?

THE GRAPHICS OF BUSINESS

Many computers that do not have "artistic" graphics do have "business" graphics, and this is what they were intended for. If your computer does not have graphics abilities, you can still use alphanumerics to produce useful graphs and charts. At the very least, the computer can prepare your data for a hand-drawn chart or graph.

There are various kinds of graphs you can use. The pie chart is used to show percentages of a whole, such as the proportion of days in the year spent on vacation, shopping, writing, collecting firewood, or in bed ill. With a pie chart, you can easily see how much of the year is spent on each activity, and thus whether you have been making the best use of your time. However, pie charts cannot be created by a computer with only minimal graphics ability, and, more importantly, you must also have a printer that can produce graphics. Given percentages and a pie-chart template, you can draw your own by hand, of course.

Bar graphs are also something of a problem, unless you have good control over your printer or have a plotter. Bar graphs can show the relative growth of corn plants given different fertilizers, or the number of people in your neighborhood with different brands of home computers. Sometimes a superimposed sequence of bar graphs is used to compare these things over time or in different places.

Scatter diagrams are relatively easy for any comput-

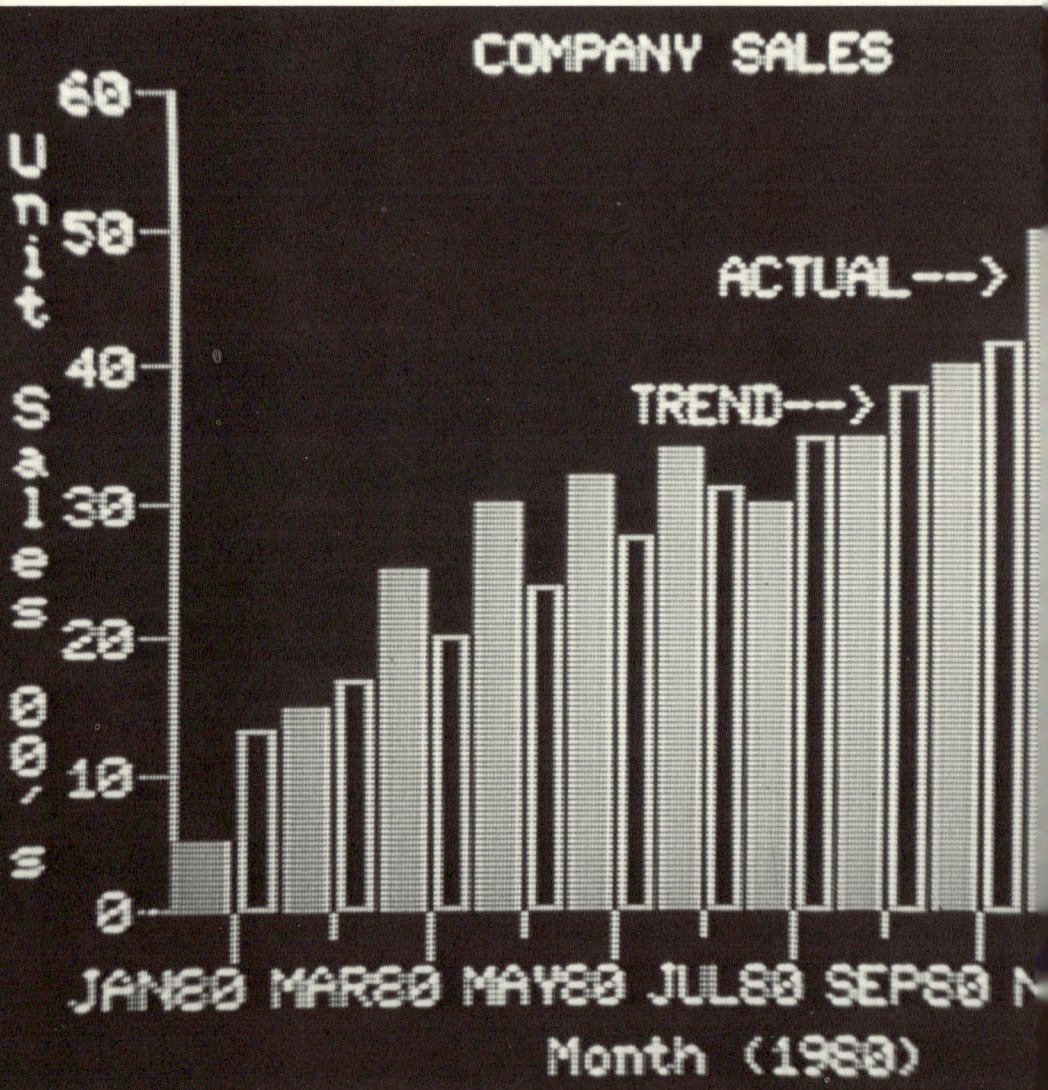

A bar graph, developed
on an Apple computer

er to produce. Each point on the diagram represents a single observation with two variables, such as how much weight a person could lift compared to his or her own weight or the number of cars passing an intersection at specific times of the day, counted over several days. Scatter diagrams are used to graph statistical information before the data has been analyzed. Astronomy's HR diagram is a scatter diagram, with the Main Sequence being the area of the greatest density of observed stars.

Of all the forms of graph, the line graph is probably the most familiar. It is what most people think of when the word "graph" is used. Line graphs are frequently used to illustrate mathematical functions, but they can also be superimposed on scatter diagrams to show correlations, if they exist, or to show stock market fluctuations over a period of time. Whether you use a line graph or a bar graph will be determined by what you intend to demonstrate. Depending on your computer's and printer's capabilities, you may have to draw in the lines between the points by hand.

In any case, the use of graphs of any form will make your data easier to understand. You should always try to represent your data graphically, and if the computer can help, so much the better.

THE BUSINESS OF GRAPHS

Graphs of any kind must be prepared with care. There are books now available, aimed at scientists and business people, as well as at students, which discuss how to properly design and draw your graphs. These are not necessarily intended for computerized display. The basic principles are simply that the graph be complete, accurately labeled, and properly scaled.

The axes of a line graph or scatter diagram should show the origin, if at all possible. If your values on the Y axis run from 50 to 75, it might seem a waste of paper to show the zero point, but cutting the graph short distorts the information it is trying to convey. If you must cut an axis, indicate the cut clearly, so that the viewer knows it has been abbreviated.

The scales of both axes should be clearly marked, and explained if necessary. To demonstrate for yourself the importance of the scale used, draw two graphs representing precipitation, one with, say, a scale of tenths of an inch, the other with whole inches, but both with the same distance between ticks. One graph is quite jagged, the other rather flat. Which one more accurately represents what you're trying to show?

Graphs, such as those used in astronomy, can also be done on logarithmic scales, but this should be clearly indicated. Do the same graph of precipitation with a log axis, to see how that changes the shape of the curve.

Graphs can be used effectively to compare data for two places or two time periods, such as places where ocean currents are warm compared to those where they are cold, to study the effect of those currents on the local climate. You plot both sets of data on the same axes, using different colors or symbols to mark the data points or lines. You should take care not to have too many lines on the same graph, however, or the graph will be unreadable.

CHARTING THE WEATHER

Meteorology is a subject that is, in itself, difficult to display at a science fair, though the results of your investigation or experiment can be shown with photographs or diagrams. Any such project will require you to collect lots of data on daily precipitation, average daily or hourly temperatures, amount and kind of cloud cover, relative humidity, wind strength and direction, dust in the air, and so on. You will probably end up with a journal filled with information, probably in tabular form. Here is an excellent opportunity to convert those tables into interesting and informative graphs.

Once you have the data collected and charted, you can then analyze it. Temperature readings taken every hour for a season or a year and graphed against season or against time of day can indicate if there is a warming or cooling trend. If you have similar data for a number of years, you can make comparisons and try to determine whether the temperature—or other variables, such as rainfall, wind force, or wind direction—remains within a constant range or is changing over time. This could be useful in determining the effects of large buildings on the movement of air in a city, for example.

Whether your data is collected from your own weather station or from published reports of global weather over a series of years, the analysis of that data is far easier to understand in graphic form.

8
SIMULATION AND MODELING

Perhaps one of the most powerful ways a computer can assist in a scientific investigation is in its ability to create simulations and models. These are mathematical rather than physical representations. The essential features of a physical, social, or abstract system or process are described mathematically in such a way that they can be manipulated to test or illustrate the effect of changes in the system.

There are a number of natural or technological processes that cannot be demonstrated easily either by a student in a laboratory or even by well-equipped research institutions. These include processes such as those requiring extremes of temperature, either far above or below what can be produced in the laboratory, and experiments involving variations in gravity. Extreme changes in velocity, or acceleration, are also not always easy to reproduce safely. In addition, some experiments involve physical components that are large and not readily available to the average student, such as bridges or skyscrapers, in the study of wind effects. The computer can be used to simulate these processes, conditions, physical laws, or objects.

LUNAR LANDER THE RIGHT WAY

By simulation we mean that we try to describe and reproduce, as far as is understood, the exact laws governing the process or system. A simulation tries to be as close to reality as possible. It is used to demonstrate how the system works and can enable people unfamiliar with the system to study it. We can vary any of the parameters within their known limits, to show how the system works under different conditions.

Running a simulation frequently shows us, when it fails to imitate what it is supposed to represent, just how little we really know about the real system. This is one of the more useful things that a computer can do, especially when the system under study is one that is hard to demonstrate physically.

The simple game *Lunar Lander* is a simulation of the reverse sort. In a real moon landing, the computer is provided with a program that controls the ship's engines to make a soft touchdown. In the game, the player simulates the computer in calculating the lander's direction and amount of thrust as it approaches the surface.

More sophisticated versions of the game allow for different gravitational fields, or for sideways movement. This makes the game more challenging as well as more realistic. In all cases, however, it is the player who is taking the part of the computer, whereas in real life the computer would make all the calculations and control the descent of the lander, following the principles incorporated into its program.

Using this as a starting point—knowing the force of gravity, the weight or mass of the lander and its fuel, the force of its thrust, the rate of fuel consumption, and so on—you could invert the game so that it is in fact the computer that is doing the calculations. This would demonstrate the amount of thrust needed as the lander descended to the surface of various real or hypothetical worlds, how that changed as the effects of gravity increased with the lander drawing nearer, how the effect of thrust changed as the lander burned fuel and lost mass, and how the gravitational forces were experienced within the vehicle.

You could design the simulation to incorporate various objectives, such as the need to descend as quickly as possible, to save as much fuel as possible, to land as gently as possible, or to land as hard as possible and still not crash. By letting the observer input the conditions he or she requires, the various kinds of landings could be demonstrated graphically, and the value of thrust, time consumed, and force of impact could be displayed as a side bar. If you also account for the effects of atmosphere, you are producing a rather sophisticated simulation and are on the verge of creating an experimental model.

IMITATIONS OF REALITY

Acceleration due to the force of gravity can easily be measured in the laboratory, at 32 ft/sec^2, or 9.8 m/sec^2. But this applies only to the earth, not to any other body in the solar system. As with the *Lunar Lander* simulation, the effects of the force of gravity on a body in the vicinity of a large mass, such as Jupiter or Mars, can be studied. These effects include perceived weight, acceleration, or the force of impact after a fall, effects that cannot be observed in the laboratory.

There is seldom room at a science fair, for example, to show the principles behind ballistics. Shooting an arrow or a bullet takes far more room than is allowed and can be dangerous, aside from the impossibility of demonstrating subtle effects. A computer simulation can show, by exaggeration, the effect of gravity, the Coriolis effect, and the effect of air friction on a projectile.

Almost any property of matter that can be quantified mathematically, such as tensile strength, hardness, or elasticity, can be simulated by a computer program. Such a simulation is most useful when either the material to be tested is not readily available, such as gold or solid oxygen, or the test might be hazardous, such as causing an explosion or heating a material to a very high temperature.

A simulated comparison is also useful when the materials to be tested are not easily made to the same dimensions, such as the tensile strengths of spider webs, brass wire, and oak. In these and other cases, a pictorial representation of what the experiment might look like, if it were actually performed, could be used to show the results of a real experiment or investigation and to show how the principles or properties involved can be applied further to other materials.

REPRESENTING THE UNKNOWN

Some laws or processes cannot be physically demonstrated at all. They are either only hypothetical, inferred from observation, or do not occur on earth. Subjects of this sort include some theories of genetics, the existence of planets orbiting other stars, the nature of the interior of a star, or the existence and behavior of quarks. These subjects can be investigated and simulated, or more properly modeled, with the help of a computer.

In mathematics, where nothing exists physically, a model is perhaps the only way we can "observe" what is going on. Four-dimensional space is hard to visualize and impossible to construct, but by means of computer graphics it can be demonstrated. Astronomy is a science in which we can do no direct experiments. We cannot change the size or position of a star, or add planets to a solar system. All we can do is observe, not actually experiment. But we can make mathematical models of what we observe.

A model embodies several principles. First, there is a

change of scale. For example, to investigate the lifting power of an airfoil, we do not need to construct a full-sized airplane and subject it to the same wind force it would encounter in a real flight. We can build a smaller version for a physical test. In real life, airfoils are frequently tested with mathematical models even before a scale model is built.

On the other hand, complex combinations of transistors and logic gates, making up part of a computer's circuitry, need not be tested in their actual microscopic size but can be—figuratively speaking—enlarged on the computer and tested before the real chip is actually designed and built.

The second principle involves a selection of specific parameters. That is, models are usually much simpler than the real thing. Only a limited number of features or selected elements—the most important according to your understanding—is actually represented. In our physical model of the stars within the solar neighborhood, we chose only to indicate the size, temperature (by color), distance, and direction of the stars. We did not include variability, interstellar radiation, dust or gas clouds, proper motion, or a host of other qualities that are known to a greater or lesser degree.

A QUESTION OF SCALE

The fact is that a model can never be a true representation of reality. But by studying the model and trying to make it come as close to reality as possible, we can learn a lot about the system under study.

We know a lot about the laws of motion governing orbiting bodies. By scaling distances down to what will fit on a computer screen, and by eliminating all considerations other than mass, distance, velocity, and the force of gravity, we can graphically represent the motion of one body around another.

One of the earliest computer games involved two spaceships orbiting a point that represented a star, a strong source of gravity. The ships applied thrust, which had a realistic effect on their motion. Inertia, acceleration, and the effect of gravity were all simulated in this game rather accurately.

In a similar fashion, you could model the earth/moon system, showing how the two bodies orbit each other. Once you have this perfected, you can use your model to explore other things. For example, how long would the lunar cycle be if the moon were 10 percent further away from the earth, or 10 percent closer? What would be the change in orbital period if the earth were 10 percent heavier, or the moon 10 percent lighter? If we include the sun in our model, can we predict when lunar or solar eclipses would occur?

To answer the above questions, the computer might be used more for numerical calculation than for graphic animation, though both are possible. The point is that you are creating a mathematical model of a physical system. How close would the moon have to come to the earth before it broke up under tidal stress? How far would it have to roam before escaping earth's gravitational field altogether? If Jupiter were where Mars is, how would that affect the earth's orbit, or the moon's orbit?

In exploring each of these questions, we are using the model to do another important thing, and that is to help make predictions. Whether the model is of a part of the solar system, or of economic systems on earth, this ability to predict the future is one of a model's most used and most important aspects. The validity of the prediction is dependent on the accuracy of the simulation and an understanding of how conditions that affect it may vary.

The more details we add to our model, the more calculations are necessary in order to make it work. Mathematical models have been used to study scientific and technological questions for centuries, but the quality of the model and its predictive ability was limited by the relatively few calculations that could be done by hand. One of the things that makes simulation and modeling so useful today is the computer's ability to manipulate large amounts of data quickly.

ENERGY AND THE EARTH

The use of computerized models can come (literally and figuratively!) down to earth with the study of energy-efficient housing. All building materials both insulate and store heat, to greater or lesser degree. Stone, for example, is a very poor insulator but holds its heat for a long time. Fiberglass, on the other hand, transmits very little heat but does not retain any. The storage and insulation qualities of any material are especially important in passive solar housing.

You can analyze your own house, to find out how well it is insulated. The exterior and interior materials must be known and compared with tables of insulating ability. The number and size of windows are counted, and whether each is single- or double-paned is determined. The type and amount of insulation in the floors, ceilings, and walls are considered, as is the direction the windows face, whether north or south, shaded or exposed. Prevailing winds and hills that protect from or funnel winds to the house also have an effect.

Once you know what your house is like, you can try creating a model to explore possible improvements. Will the addition of another inch (2.5 cm) of fiberglass insulation pay off, when its cost is compared with the cost of fuel? After all, past a certain point you get diminishing returns. In your climate is electric, gas, or wood heat most efficient? What happens if you change the color of the roofing material? The effects of moisture barriers can sometimes make a difference, as can attic ventilation fans.

When it comes to solar heat, there are a number of

alternatives. In many cases, your model will help decide whether the cost of construction can be paid back over a reasonable period of time in reduced heating bills. But summer cooling is another thing. Here, window awnings, or trees, are alternatives to air conditioning.

Heat pumps can use either air or water as a source or dump of heat. Given your local climate and the availability of groundwater, what kind of heat pump would be best for you, or indeed, would one work in your area at all?

One of the more interesting possible solutions to energy-efficient housing is the underground house. Rock and soil are poor insulators, but they retain heat (or cold) for extended periods of time. If you were to design an underground house, how would you place the windows, if there were any at all? An earth-sheltered house can be completely below grade, or have earth drawn up over it in a berm. It can have an atrium, or just a south-facing window wall. Once you have figured out the mathematical representations of such things as thermal mass, insulation, exposure, and insolation in summer and winter, you can construct a model to help you design an earth-sheltered home to provide you with the kind of living environment you desire.

FORECASTING THE WEATHER

Meteorological studies involve the acquisition of large amounts of data using certain instruments, such as a barometer, a hydrometer, a wind meter, and so on. The information these instruments provide can be recorded by means of pens (plotters) on paper. They are analog information, constantly changing reflections in ink of the conditions they measure. The meanings of the numbers cannot be understood until the data has been analyzed in a number of ways to try to find some pattern or significance. Without a computer, modern weather forecasting—as inaccurate as it so often is—would not exist.

If you have several years worth of data on weather

patterns, including insolation (the amount of sunlight received), ozone effects, evaporation, wind cycles, and so on, you can construct a model to demonstrate roughly how global weather works. For example, dust in the air and snow on the ground both affect how much of the light that reaches the orbit of the earth is actually received by the earth, and how much is reflected or lost by reradiation. The more detail you can add, the closer your model will come to being a simulation, though a true simulation of the entire system is not possible with our present degree of understanding.

You can use your meteorological model to explore some interesting possibilities. For example, what would happen to our climate if the ozone layer were reduced or increased? Our use of fluorocarbons in spray cans is thought to be one possible mechanism whereby this could happen. But people aren't the only causers of pollution. A volcano such as El Chichón throws tons of dust into the air, as well as gases containing highly active or polluting chemicals. Some of these may or may not increase the Greenhouse Effect. How does an eruption like that of El Chichón or of Mount St. Helens affect our weather? How much dust would it take to reduce the annual average temperature by one degree?

Even clouds affect our weather, as we all know, and sometimes in ways that surprise us. Can you explain how clouds cool the day by reflecting light, or warm the night by keeping heat in? Clouds may have only a day-to-day effect, but what might our weather be like if the axial tilt of our planet were different? Would that change be greater or lesser than if we were just a bit closer to or further from the sun? We bring astronomy here right down to earth.

One of the important things about a model is that its parameters—constants to which we assign different values—are things about which we know little, or which we would like to change to see the consequences. A large number of factors go into cloud formation, for example, such as dust, temperature, mixing of air at various levels, and so on. As a cloud forms it might simply hold the moisture or let it fall as rain or snow. By changing the values of these parameters, we hope to learn more about how rain can be induced to fall when and where we want it.

Simulation and modeling so frequently go together that both subjects are often discussed at the same time. In your projects, you can emphasize one aspect or the other—a simulation of what is known or a model to explore the unknown. Your project will usually include both aspects.

Designing a simulation or model is not easy, and there are dozens of highly technical books on the subject. It will also take a lot of research into the system you wish to model or simulate. Computer programs of this sort can be as trivial as illustrating a bouncing ball or as complex as the immense programs that (almost) simulate the processes of human thought.

FUTURE EVOLUTION

Genetic experiments can sometimes take years to complete. Although the results make a good display, sometimes the experiment must be passed over by the typical student, since the time involved is too great. Given knowledge of certain principles, however, such as those involving the acquisition of a mutation and passing it on to offspring, a computer can simulate such experiments. This simulation can be used instead of an actual experiment, or it can be used to augment a real one.

Mutations are in large part very subtle and not always easily proven to exist. It is an accumulation of many small mutations that result in gross changes in physiology and anatomy. All evolution is merely the culmination of millions of tiny—and sometimes not so tiny—changes in the form and function of a living species.

If our population is of fruit flies, which produce

hundreds of offspring every few weeks, we can follow the effects of a natural or induced mutation through the generations. If we have more time, as dog breeders do, we can study the progress of selected traits, such as size or color, though perfecting a new breed might take a century or more. Corn, or maize, produces a new generation every year, and we can try to select for natural mutations for higher protein content or disease resistance, as well as cross-breed for these traits.

In all these cases, considerable research is done before the actual experiment, and the scientist or breeder must be aware of other factors, such as environment, nutrition, competition, unexpected mutation, and so on, which can affect and confuse the study. With beans or fruit flies, you can perform a real-life genetic study, but some questions are best investigated with a model.

Suppose, for example, that a mutation occurs once every ten offspring—or once every hundred. Families (whether human or animal) average a certain size, and reproduction occurs every so often. By assigning these and other parameters different values, and relating them to each other mathematically, we can create a model that will let us explore when a particular mutation will either become permanent or disappear.

If the mutation is dominant, or if it is recessive, how does that affect the results? If the population is very small and inbred, or if it is large, with a lot of mixing of the gene pool, how will that assure a permanent mutation? If the mutation enhances or hinders reproduction or growth, how will that affect its spread? What kind of conditions can cause a recessive harmful mutation, such as sickle-cell anemia, to continue to spread? If mutation occurs more frequently, if reproduction occurs more often, or if the number of offspring increases, can the mutation continue to spread in spite of being harmful, or will it destroy the population?

In this model, we are studying not a specific trait but

the actual process and spread of a mutation or genetic difference. Studies of the behavior of individual animals make best use of the computer's ability to store and manipulate data. The study of whole systems, on the other hand, is more amenable to modeling and simulation.

If we were to try a long-term mutation experiment with humans or any other long-lived or slowly reproducing species, such a study would take decades or centuries, if it could be done at all. And although models of such experiments could be explored on paper, the computer allows us to examine the development of the mutation over many generations, in large populations, in a short period of time, and using a larger number of variables, many of which are difficult to allow for or control in the field.

BALANCE IN NATURE

Another area in which it is sometimes easier to study a model than the actual system itself is ecology, which is the study of how animals and plants interact with each other and their environment. To do a successful study in this area, of course, much field work must have been previously done, large amounts of data collected, individual animals studied, and some statistical inferences made.

Ecology is a popular topic of discussion and investigation today. We have learned that killing the mountain lion does not help the deer population, and that dumping stuff in water does not throw it away; it merely kills the fish and comes back to us in our drinking supply. The whole world is a complex ecological experiment, and in our studies we can usually investigate only small portions of the whole. Thus we are back to modeling again.

For example, in a forest environment, a full study of all the variables might be impossible, or at least extremely time-consuming and costly to do. But we could select certain elements for a more limited model. Given data as to the availability of certain kinds of plant life, used as food by rabbits and mice, and the number of predators, such as foxes and wolves, we could construct a model that not only explores how all these interact—and how the situation changes as, say, the wolves are destroyed or the rabbits overbreed—but also explores animal behavior.

There is the additional possibility of turning such a model into an educational game. For example, you can put the player in the role of a member of one of the species, to test his or her choices against what is known about the interrelation of the species. Could the person, as a mouse or an owl, survive? Should a rabbit meeting a wolf run, hide, freeze, or pay no attention? The possibilities of exploration, expansion, and variation on this theme are almost limitless. And by putting the model into the form of a fantasy role-playing game, we can not only investigate ecological principles, to see how they work, but also teach them to others.

DYNAMIC NEIGHBORHOOD

Let us consider a different kind of example, the *Game of Life*, which is played on graph paper. Spots on the squares "live" or "die" according to how many neighbors they have, and empty squares acquire new spots if population conditions are right. In its early stages, the game can easily be played with pencil and paper. But sometimes Life can go on for generations and can cover huge areas of paper. Then it is almost impossible to accurately make each generation by hand. That is when an effort spent on developing a program to follow the same rules and display the game on the screen would pay off.

One social process similar in some ways to the *Game of Life* is the segregation of neighborhoods. Although this model would follow slightly different and more sophisticated rules, it could be demonstrated on a computer in much the same way that Life is demonstrated. A full presentation would require supplementary materials, specifying the varying initial conditions and "comfort" requirements of the population.

One starts with a definition of "neighbor" as someone who lives on either side of you, or across the street or directly behind your house—diagonal neighbors are ignored for simplicity's sake. The initial mixture of two ethnic groups—again only two for simplicity's sake—can be random, even, or biased in some way.

One then decides what people are "comfortable" with: all neighbors of the same ethnic group as the individual, at least two neighbors the same, at least one the same, or they don't care. Each group can have different preferences. Then one assumes that people will move to a more comfortable situation every so often. Account will have to be taken for people moving out of the neighborhood altogether or moving in from outside, and for some residences being left empty.

Under what circumstances will a neighborhood automatically segregate itself? Is it possible to change the outcome by changing the initial mixture? What happens if one group is more tolerant of strangers than the other? How does vacant property affect the distribution? What happens if you have three groups?

A model such as the above is extremely simplified. We did not consider political persuasion, education, economic status, the changes in any of these over time, or any of the other variables of human culture. Like the *Game of Life,* we considered only the need for like neighbors. Still, such a model has validity, as long as its limitations and simplicity are taken into account.

Starting with a population living in an area of twenty by twenty lots, in our segregation model, you could test any set of conditions by hand only a few times before errors and fatigue set in. A computer program can run until you shut it off or a stable condition results.

By selecting only one or two variables and initial conditions, we can model other social phenomena in the same way. The first and greatest problem is to select the specific condition or variable to be tested, and then to create a mathematical method that will represent it. If you find this kind of model interesting, or games like the *Game of Life* fascinating, get a copy of the book *Laws of the Game* by Manfred Eigen and Ruthild Winkler, published in the United States in 1981 by Alfred A. Knopf.

MAKING MONEY

Economics is a special area of social behavior, and a complex one. Economic models are likely to be graphic, in the sense of graphs and charts, rather than pictorial.

The computer provides the ability to do a large number of repetitious calculations, as well as complex calculations, and can also introduce a random factor if desired, such as fluctuations in material prices and number of customers. There are a number of commercially available computer games that, in only slightly different form, would be good models of rather complex economic processes.

One of the simplest of economic models is the Lemonade Stand, frequently presented as a game for children. The object of the game is to stay in business and make a profit. Cost of materials, price of product, initial funds, and customer demand are the components modeled. As simple as it is, it shares features with many sophisticated economic models. The game can be used as the foundation for more complex studies.

The important point here is that we do not know enough about the economics of even so simple a system as a child's lemonade stand to be able to create a full simulation. We can't predict how many people will pass by, how thirsty they will be, how much money they will have, how much of a hurry they will be in, and so on.

All these, as well as other unknowns, will have an effect on the success or failure of the Lemonade Stand.

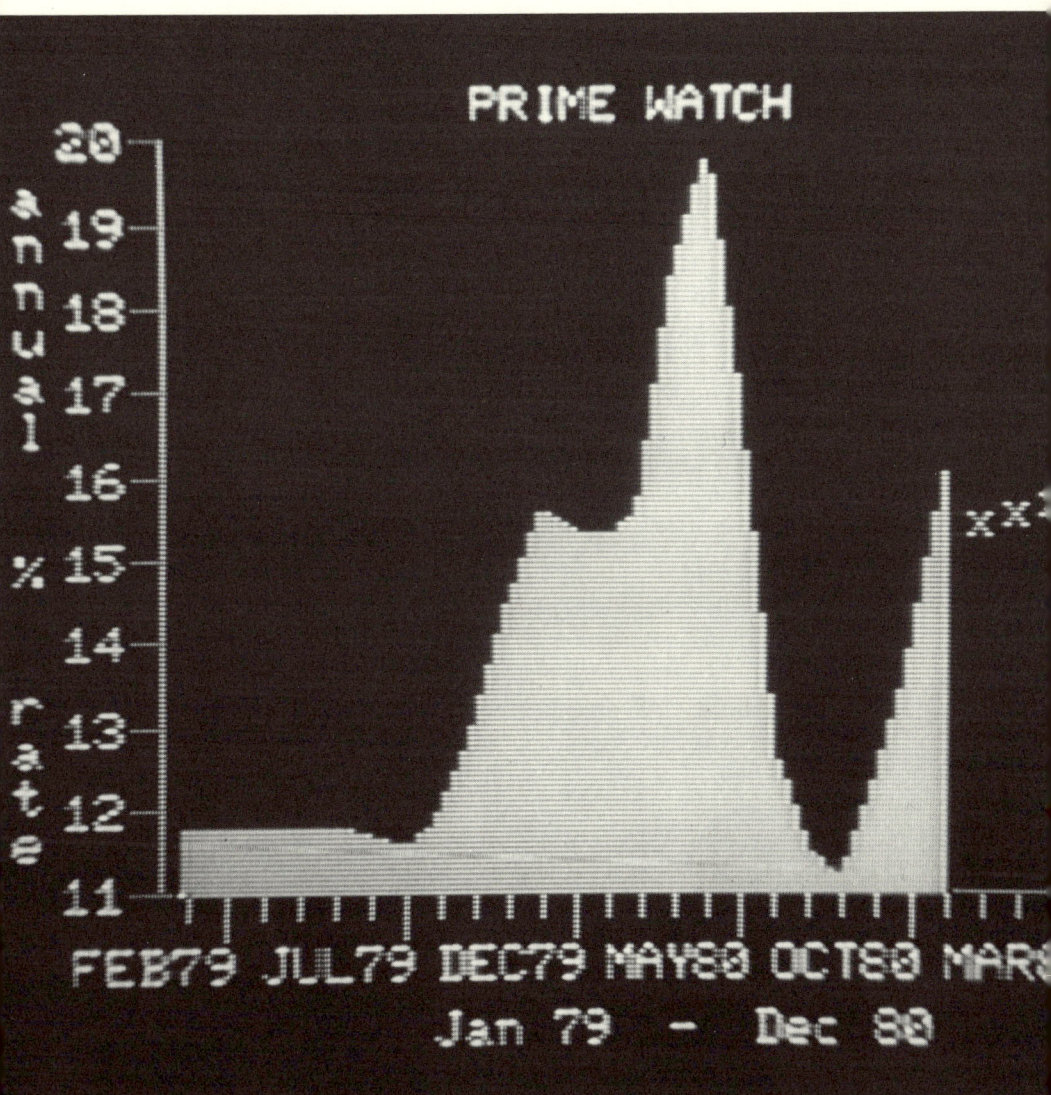

Economic models often take the
form of graphs or charts.
These have more impact than long
lists of numbers or many pages of text.

Some, such as waiting to buy the ingredients on sale, or varying the recipe to reduce cost, are pretty much under our control. Others are not, and we can only make guesses as to how things will work, or how we think they should work. By studying a model, we can learn more about the system, until we can at last simulate it accurately.

As said earlier, one of the main uses of economic models is to try to predict the future—forecasting. How will the economy change if federal spending increases or decreases? If spending increases, should it be on futuristic projects such as the space program or social programs such as welfare? If a particular item of the budget is cut, what effect will it have on the rest of the economy or in reduced income for the people cut, who will then reduce their spending? What happens to the value of money when more is printed, less is printed, or the money is tied up in investments and savings or replaced by credit?

Questions like these confound the experts, though simple models might be constructed to make preliminary investigations. The accuracy of the prediction may be questionable, but the value of even amateur efforts at constructing models of even parts of the economy can be of real benefit. Your work with a Lemonade Stand today could pay off for you in the future.

BALANCING THE BOOKS

Programs that perform "spreadsheet" calculations are models of mathematical systems designed for examining a particular class of economic situations. You need not write your own spreadsheet program in order to use one to help investigate some very complex problems. When these kinds of calculations were done by hand, they were extremely time-consuming and subject to critical errors. Yet even the simplest of these programs is a powerful tool.

Politics is another area where computer modeling can be quite informative. Here it is used to help predict the results of elections, the needs of the electorate, and sensitivity to certain issues. Politics, like business, is more an art than a science, but it is still amenable to modeling, forecasting, and statistical analysis. Converting what you have learned into a computerized display, whether your display is a pictorial model or a series of charts and graphs, can give the observer a better understanding of what you have accomplished.

9
COMPUTER CONTROL OF OTHER DEVICES

Computers can be used to control other devices that you might want to use in your project. We mention this only in passing, as the problems of interfacing and writing drivers for these devices is beyond the scope of this book. However, if a robot is available, or if you have built one of your own, computer control of the robot would make a good demonstration. The robot itself could be the project, of course.

Perhaps not obvious to everyone is the fact that CRTs, disk or tape drives, printers, and other peripherals are rather complex robotic devices under computer control. In a way, a moving graphic image is a "light-robot." If you are knowledgeable about computer hardware, you could demonstrate just how these peripherals respond to computer instructions.

One possible demonstration of computer control could be using a computer to direct the movements of a model train—stopping, starting, backing up, switching turnouts, and so on—around a small layout. Such control could either be by program or by direct command at a keyboard. Sensors under the tracks could also keep tabs on where the train is at any given moment and perhaps record its real and scale speed. If you are into model trains, such a project could be of more than momentary interest to you.

Most of the sensors that input data are analog in nature. They measure light, sound, or position in a continuum. Computers today, for the most part, use digital information, measurements reduced to discrete numbers instead of being continuously variable. Thus, analog information must be converted to digital before the computer can use it.

One of the simplest and most common of analog input devices is the joystick or game paddle. An inexpensive one can be taken apart to show what it looks like inside. Then, perhaps using computer graphics, you can show how the signals from the joystick or paddle are converted into digital data. Most computer games use a joystick to move an image around on the screen. Can you write a simple demonstration program that does just this? More importantly, can you explain how it works?

The construction of instruments that do analog-to-digital conversion and the creation of software to support them would be good projects in and of themselves. When computers control other devices, the instructions frequently have to be converted back from digital to analog. How is this done?

Measurements of speed, velocity, and acceleration frequently require the use of a stopwatch or other timing device. The problem with a stopwatch is that it depends on human reaction time and can measure only relatively large fractions of a second. To measure the time of, say, a model car moving along a track, you could take the firing buttons from two joysticks and mount them under the track in such a way that the weight of the car will depress them, sending a signal to the computer. When the first signal is received, the computer starts timing; it stops when the car passes over the second button. This eliminates almost all human error in time measurement.

A common computer input device
is the joystick.
Can you explain how it works?

A PSYCHOLOGICAL EXPERIMENT

You can use a computer to help you to conduct your experiment in other ways, too. Even without sophisticated hardware peripherals, the visual display of a CRT can help, especially when you are dealing with other people, as in some of the basic kinds of psychology experiments run by beginning students.

The subject sits in a completely darkened room, facing a computer terminal located about 10 feet (3 m) away. Absolutely nothing is visible in the room except for the two tiny dots of light, perhaps 4 or 5 inches (10 or 12 cm) apart, on the CRT. The terminal is carefully mounted on a wheeled platform so that it can be moved toward or away from the subject in such a way that the subject cannot hear it move. The dots of light can also be made to move closer together or farther apart, under simple program control, possibly from a separate keyboard. It is important that the subject be able to see only the dots, nothing else.

The object of the experiment is to test the perception of distance. The experimenter sometimes moves the terminal closer to the subject, then further away. At other times, he or she moves the dots slightly closer together, then further apart. After each test, the experimenter asks whether the terminal has moved or the dots have moved.

COLOR, SHAPE, AND SOUND

Some computers can produce fine gradations of color, brightness, or both. The values can be accurately specified as variables in the program. In this way, you can test for perception of color or brightness.

If a red circle is surrounded by a green background, for example, the circle looks very red indeed. If it is surrounded by a purple background, it looks more orange. This change of apparent color can be demonstrated with either a change of the background color or the circle color. If two spots of the same color are placed on backgrounds of different colors at the same time, can the subject tell they are the same? If different, can he or she tell that?

Two areas of color placed close together sometimes produce what appears to be a band of a different color between them. (With some color monitors, this band is really there and is not an illusion.) What color combinations cause the strongest effect? How close do the colors have to be to produce it? Some computers use this effect, called "dithering," to produce more colors than normally available. A very fine-grained checkerboard of two different colors is displayed, and from a normal viewing distance, it looks likes a third color is present.

We see horizontal lines differently from vertical lines. A computer with high-resolution graphics can demonstrate this perception, to show how closely packed lines can be distinguished more easily in one orientation or another. How about diagonal lines? Optical illusions involving lines crossing each other can also be produced in the same way.

Many computers have sound-generating capabilities. Frequently, such sounds are so similar in pitch as to be indistinguishable from one another. Also, the volume of the sound can be precisely controlled. Tests of audio perception and discrimination can be developed using these facilities.

One of the standard tests of memory is to present the subject with a series of random numbers or nonsense syllables. The computer can create these numbers or syllables according to any scheme you desire. It can also present them on the screen for precisely timed durations and at precise intervals. It can redisplay them in any order desired. As in the popular *Simon* game, sounds can also be presented in series, with the subject trying to duplicate them.

THE ASSISTANT COMPUTER

Conducting tests and experiments of this sort, without the aid of a computer, would require the making of special equipment. Unless constructed very carefully, the quality of the equipment, if not very good, can invalidate the results of the test. The computer itself is all the special equipment you need.

In the first test of perception just described, the answers the subject gives must be recorded. But notes taken in the dark can be illegible, and in any case they must later be keyed in and analyzed. If, instead of simply answering, "nearer, further, closer, apart," the subject could touch keys, each answer would be automatically recorded. A joystick could be used to move color squares closer together until the illusion of a varying band between them appeared.

The computer's ability to function as a stopwatch can be taken advantage of in psychological experiments, too. This can ensure that the length of time a subject is exposed to a stimulus is always the same and not dependent on the experimenter, who might introduce a bias by inadvertently letting one person see, say, a random number longer than he or she shows it to another. The computer can time responses within a few hundredths or a few thousandths of a second, though that degree of accuracy might not be necessary. The computer can also keep track of correct responses as opposed to incorrect ones, without the chance of the experimenter misunderstanding a verbal answer. And then, after the experiment is over, the results are already in the computer, to be analyzed in whatever way is appropriate and printed out without having to be typed by the experimenter.

10

COMPUTER SOUND

Computers can make sounds as well as pictures. Except for sophisticated music synthesizers, however, sound has been a relatively neglected part of computer use. Today we are seeing more and more sound-producing capabilities on the newer machines. Computers can not only make sounds—even music—they can also synthesize voice, are beginning to be able to recognize voices, and can be used to analyze and model the acoustical properties of buildings, instruments, and speakers. Computers can also help in the control of recordings, and in the teaching of music.

Computerized music has a long way to go, though the state of the art today, even with inexpensive home computers, is encouraging and promises considerable abilities in the not-too-distant future. Anyone interested in music should find something of interest here.

Computers with the proper equipment can be made to "play" almost any piece of music, according to specific instructions for the pitch and duration of each note in its program. There have also been some experiments in programming a computer to "compose" its own simple melodies, by choosing notes randomly but following rules of melody and harmonics. If you can write a similar program yourself, you can demonstrate your understanding of the musical styles of classical composers, such as Bach or Beethoven, by having the computer create music in their style.

THE COMPUTER AS MUSICAL INSTRUMENT

When two notes are played together, they produce harmonics or chords. Two notes very close to each other, "out of tune" with each other, produce a beat, or throbbing sound. Chords made up of three or more notes are sometimes very similar but have a different "feel," as between major and minor. Usually one note defines the chord by dominating, such as C-sharp. These concepts can be demonstrated audibly, of course, but they can also be shown visually at the same time by means of notes on a staff. Can you use a similar method to show the difference between various keys or modes?

When a note is produced, it has several characteristics. Among these are attack and decay—how quickly the note reaches maximum volume and how long it takes to return to silence. Also, while the note is played, it can either be sustained or have tremolo. The actual shape of the note can be shown, like a complicated sine wave. This represents the fundamental sound and overtones. Some computerized music systems allow you to modify this directly, by using a light pen or by programming values into variables. Thus, not only the pitch of the note but also its quality—whether it sounds like a bassoon or a trumpet—can be controlled. If your computer has this capability, how many different instruments can you imitate? Can you show by means of the graphic sound wave how and why a violin and a flute sound different?

More familiar musical instruments produce notes by the vibration of a membrane (drums), a string (guitar), or a column of air (clarinet). The physical shape of the instrument, the materials of which it is made, and the nature of the sound-producing element contribute to the kind of note produced. Pitch and overtones can be graphically demonstrated by the vibration of a plucked string. An organ pipe's sound varies not only with size but also with shape and material. Fingering the holes of a piccolo changes the pitch of the note. Can you use computer graphics to show how all these things work? If your computer can take music from a microphone, can it be programmed to display the note played on a guitar? Can it reproduce the shape of the sound?

Computers can also be used in the teaching of music. The screen and a pianolike keyboard, working together, can help a student learn scales or simple melodies, by leading him or her through the finger movements with a graphic representation of the keyboard on the screen. The computer indicates which key should be played or which one actually was played. Relating the piano keyboard to the notes on a musical staff can help in learning how to read music.

A NONHUMAN VOICE

Besides making music, computers are being used today to study and simulate the human voice. One of the more interesting areas of study is the physiology of the human mouth, tongue, teeth, and throat, which enable us to produce the thousands of sounds that make up verbal language. Chimpanzees, as has been demonstrated, have different oral structures, which prevent them from acquiring vocal language, though symbolic or gestural language may be a possibility for them. Programs that graphically show how the tongue, teeth, lips, and throat shape sounds are being used to help people with certain kinds of speech problems.

When a computer synthesizes a voice, however, it does not attempt to reproduce the sound using techniques humans normally use. Instead, it employs the same technology used in radios and stereos. That is, it vibrates a speaker cone, trying to simulate the same acoustical wave patterns that a human voice does. The human voice, besides producing a tone, also has qualities of sibilance, stopping, aspiration, and so on.

Computers are already being used, by the phone company and others, to send voice messages. They usually do this by selecting prerecorded words and phrases from tape, and combining them to form (somewhat) meaningful sentences. Or, a word can be spoken and recorded digitally. This digital information can then be stored as any other computer information is and used to drive speakers or a telephone handset.

At the same time, much attention is being focused on how to construct words from basic sounds. With the various inexpensive voice-synthesizer peripherals available now to the home computer user, you can do much to increase your understanding of sound or music.

11

INSIDE THE COMPUTER

In order to take advantage of a computer in the preparation, analysis, and display of any science project, you will have to know at least a modicum of practical computer science. Even if your major area of scientific interest is something else, however, if you're reading this book, you're interested in computers, too. And, of course, the computer itself is an excellent subject for a science project, whether the project be practical or theoretical. We cannot go very deeply into theoretical computer science here. That requires years of study and training, and frequently rather expensive resources. Also, as we said at the beginning, we will not explore what is possible in the way of hardware construction projects.

How computers use information and follow instructions is a subject worthy of some research. Each bit of information is stored in a memory location and passes through logic gates. We cannot actually see memory in operation, at least not directly, nor can we directly demonstrate the functioning of registers and I/O ports. However, by use of a graphic simulation that reflects the contents of memory or the functions of circuits, we can show what goes on inside a computer when we use it.

Can you set up a graphic model of a series of gates designed to do a simple calculation, and show how different input has different effects and results? How are data and commands stored in memory, what does an address mean, and what are the contents of an address? By using either hand-drawn pictures and diagrams or computer graphics, show what a physical bit of memory might look like if magnified sufficiently.

SEEING IT IN ACTION

What you just drew is a representation of the most basic of machine operations. Can you also explain and demonstrate how the accumulator works, and how the other registers in a computer work? Again, use graphic rather than verbal methods, whether hand- or computer-drawn, though a detailed written description should accompany the program.

A monitor is a program that does just this, but usually by displaying a series of addresses and their contents, either in binary, hexadecimal, or decimal notation, and sometimes their ASCII equivalents. By use of a monitor, one can trace a program as it is running and examine, after each operation or change of state, the contents of the various registers and flags.

Write a simple monitor to display memory, registers, and flag contents. This should show what is actually going on inside the computer when a simple program is running. If possible, can you convert the monitor display from hex notation into graphic images of the registers themselves as the program is run? Use this monitor to explain the program that is running, as well as to explain how the CPU works.

Write a monitor that monitors itself, graphically if possible, while it is responding to user input. The idea is to show directly how the computer works, not on a separate program but on itself.

PROGRAMMING ILLUSTRATED

All computer instructions are in the form of a program. Although inside the machine these instructions take the form of binary electronic pulses, the days of machine-language programming are nearly past. The first improvement in writing programs was assembly language, in which each machine-language instruction, composed of a string of zeros and ones, was given a simple mnemonic code, a group of letters that, it was hoped, reminded the programmer what the instruction was supposed to do. Assembly language still gives the programmer direct control over the registers, their contents, and the contents of each address of memory, just as machine language does. The program that converts assembly language to machine instructions is quite sophisticated and was the beginning of the language revolution.

Once a program is written, no matter what the language, it must be run. Each language runs in its own way. What happens when a program is run—not at machine level but at a higher level? In other words, rather than showing what happens in registers, memory locations, and logic gates, show what each line does.

For example, what happens when the computer encounters the BASIC command **GOTO?** Can you show this with a cursor moving down the lines of the program as the instruction is carried out on the screen? When an **IF-THEN** statement is executed, can you show graphically just what happens? How about **FOR-NEXT** or **ON-GOSUB?** The object is to show how control flows through the program, how loops work, and how decisions are made.

Programs use variables and constants. What is the difference between them and the significance of each? What is the difference between integer, real, and string variables? This gets into the area of memory storage and addressing again, but differently from before. Some languages, such as FORTH, use a stack. What is it, and how does it work?

Programs have to be carefully designed and algorithms written. Then the programs have to be tested and debugged. The problems here are due in large part to the strictness of computer logic compared to the ambiguities of human thought.

To help us in the design and debugging of programs, we use flowcharts, which illustrate the larger logic of the language, the decisions made, and the flow of control. Explain a flowchart, each of the symbols used, and how a flowchart helps us keep track of what a program is doing. If you have computer graphics, can you write a program that demonstrates itself or another program with flowchart symbols? In other words, as the program runs, when you come to an input box, let the user put something in—a name or a decision. Then go step by step through the consequential boxes, perhaps with color enhancement, to show that a flowchart is not just a pretty picture but a symbolic representation of the actual running of the program.

COMPARATIVE PROGRAMMING

Demonstrate by means of two different programs that accomplish the same thing the differences between one that is efficient and well written and one that uses brute force or is poorly written or designed. Here you can show how certain computer "tricks" work—and how the use of these can also mislead or confuse someone who is trying to understand your program by reading the listing.

Programs, if not in machine language, are in some higher-level language. Each high-level language was designed for a different purpose. Each has its own strengths and weaknesses and is more or less similar to other languages in some ways, different in other ways. The reasons for these variations are not always clear to the average person—or to the average user.

Write a simple program, such as to add two numbers or print the user's name on the screen, in a high-level lan-

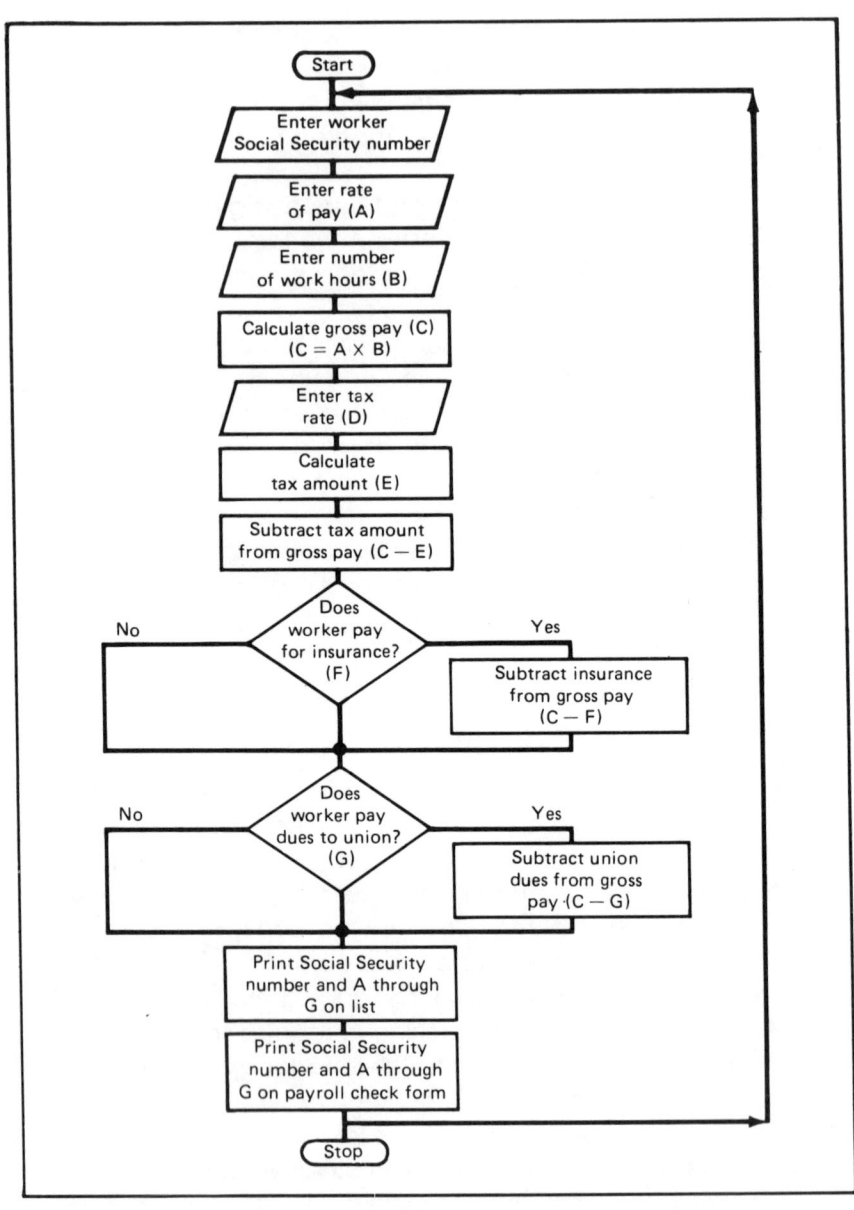

An example of a flowchart

guage such as BASIC or Pascal. Then write a program in assembly language that does the same thing. If you know how your interpreter or compiler works, show how each high-level command, statement, or function is a set of assembly instructions that, taken together, are larger than a direct assembly program that accomplishes the same thing.

Use your best (short) assembly program and write it out in machine code, either in hex or binary or both. This shows how difficult it was for the earliest programmers to write and understand machine-language programs and to debug them. Your comparison should probably be presented in the reverse order, that is, the machine program first, the improvement to assembly mnemonics next, and the version in a high-level language last. The program you use as your example need not run on the machine, but it should exemplify the differences between the three levels.

A BABEL OF LANGUAGES

High-level languages are usually either interpreted or compiled. These two methods give a different feel to the use of the language and have different effects on editing, speed of the run, and so on. Write a program in two similar languages, such as BASIC and Pascal, or interpreted and compiled versions of BASIC, so that the program listings are as identical as possible. Then, by charts and diagrams, show the differences between the two. Demonstrate how one runs faster than the other. Also demonstrate how the compilation process can add to the time needed to prepare small programs, or how modularity improves the ease of debugging large programs. Can you explain why, under certain circumstances, one would be preferable to the other? FORTH is, in a way, both interpreted and compiled, as are a few other languages. Explain how that works.

BASIC and Pascal are quite similar in some ways and quite different in others, aside from being interpreted or compiled. Can you demonstrate those differences and the different philosophies inherent in the design of each? Can you defend both philosophies?

Other languages are more or less similar to BASIC and Pascal, both descendants of FORTRAN, though Pascal has ALGOL in its ancestry, too. COBOL is rather different, in that it is much more specialized and can do certain things much better than BASIC can and other things less well. Is it possible to write a program in COBOL to use color graphics? Can you use extensive string variables in FORTRAN? PILOT is another language that, like COBOL, was designed with a special purpose in mind. Can you show why PILOT has greater power and ease of use in some areas, and is less powerful or less useful in others?

Other languages are quite different. The logic of APL is similar to that of more familiar languages, but its listings bear no resemblance to BASIC or Pascal at all. FORTH and C, on the other hand, are in another family altogether. How are they and other threaded interpretive languages different from the more familiar BASIC and Pascal? One thing, of course, is that these last languages allow the user to modify the language itself.

LISP and other list processing, or "actor," languages fall in still another family. The logic of LISP is markedly different from that of Pascal, in that Pascal makes quite clear distinctions between program and data, and between kinds of data, while LISP makes no distinction whatsoever. Can you make this clear to someone unfamiliar with the language? What makes LOGO, a language derived from LISP, special?

There is considerable effort under way today to make programming a computer easier. Part of this involves using more Englishlike commands. This can be done by writing the language so that common words and phrases are built in, or by writing a "shell" that enables an existing language to understand Englishlike commands. Both strategies are being pursued. Can you write a simple language or shell to allow the user to use a few simple but purely English commands and get results in English? As a clue, the popular adventure-type games, written in either assembly or BASIC, use a parser, a subprogram that translates English words and phrases into computer instructions. Here we are getting into the area of human-language simulation and artificial intelligence.

12

ODDS AND ENDS

We have hardly touched on the many possible ways you can use a computer in a science project, whether for a school-sponsored science fair or for your own pleasure. Collected here are a few ideas that didn't quite belong in any of the previous chapters.

For example, some of the most intriguing psychological studies being carried out today are in the area of artificial intelligence. Articles in the popular computing and science magazines indicate the degree of sophistication involved, as well as how far we yet have to go before we truly understand what intelligence is and how to simulate it. The classic program ELIZA is a rather simple example of what can be done. Here is another area where any studies or insights you have may be of real significance.

ELECTRONIC PLAY

A rather specialized but economically important area of computer science is electronic, arcade, and computer games. There is no denying that these games have captured the imaginations of many people. A game, just for its own sake, would probably not make a very good science project, though many people might play it. However, a game can be used to demonstrate almost any topic, especially models and simulations.

To make a good science project, a game does not necessarily have to be "educational," though that would help. The principles of interaction with the computer and explanations or demonstrations of how the program works are important. The game format could make the presentation of other topics more interesting and informative.

Of course, if you choose to demonstrate your project or its results with a game, you will have to master completely the arts of interactive programming and error-trapping. More than any other form of computer display, a game should be self-operating, without the player having to ask the designer how to do things. If the program crashes, interest in the game will evaporate immediately.

Although designing a game, in and of itself, is quite a task, when you want to use a game to illustrate something, you have the additional design problem of how best to represent that information in the context of the game. When the players have finished, they should not only have enjoyed themselves, they should also have learned something.

Study educational games you have played, to see how information is presented. Study other games as well, to see what makes them interesting to play. This is one of the biggest problems with educational gaming—many are downright dull. A "game" that merely simulates flash-cards, simply asks questions, or only displays text or information is not a game.

Game theory is a special branch of mathematics that can benefit from the use of a computer. Some games, such as tic-tac-toe, are "solved," that is, a known strategy exists that guarantees the first player a win, or at least a draw. Show what that strategy is. Other games are more complex, involving the theories of formal strategy, minimax, saddle points, and so on. These are amenable to both mathematical solution and graphic representation.

Computers can be taught to play highly complex games, such as Chess. The Chess program shown being developed here, called Belle, could beat all but the very best human Chess champions. Can you write a simple game program for your computer?

INPUT

In order for the computer to control anything, whether it be a printer or a robot, signals must go out from it to the device controlled, and information on the status of the device must come back to the computer. The information passing through the ports, in one direction or the other, must also be regulated and controlled. How can you demonstrate this?

Instructions from the keyboard are translated into signals that the computer can recognize, and there are limits to just how many such signals there are. What are these limits, and why do they exist? There are various arrangements of keyboards other than the one with which we are familiar, though they transmit the same codes, for the most part. Explain what you know about these arrangements, and why you might prefer one over another.

One particular device for controlling the screen image is a light pen. Some people think the pen actually sends a beam of light to the screen. Can you explain how it really works, and write a program to demonstrate some of its uses and peculiarities? There are also touch-sensitive screens these days, using one of at least two principles: actual conductors embedded in the glass front, or infrared or laser photocells arranged around the sides. How do these work, what are their limitations, and to what special purposes might they be put?

CRTs AND OTHER SCREENS

How does a computer put an image on the screen? By constructing a model of a cutaway CRT—or by actually having one cut in half—can you show its working parts and use supplementary diagrams to show how the electron gun works and how an image is formed by a raster scan? If the CRT produces color, you can add to your project something on the principles of additive color. By magnifying the image of an actual CRT, or by well-drawn pictures, perhaps you can show the dot-matrix format of screen characters. Vector graphics is another form of screen imaging, used in some arcade games and even in some models of home electronic games. Explain how that is different from raster scan CRTs.

LCD (Liquid Crystal Display) watches have been around for a long time, and the technique is now beginning to be used to produce flat monitor screens, especially for pocket and small portable computers. Liquid crystals are also used for other purposes, such as temperature monitors. Even if you don't have an LCD, you can explore the possibilities of their use. For example, can LCD be used for producing color displays? What are the power requirements or limits to resolution compared to a CRT screen?

There are other technologies for reducing the size of a monitor screen. Each has its own drawbacks as well as advantages. Can you explain or demonstrate these? They could be used for pocket TVs as well as pocket computers, and there's the possibility of further research here. Other considerations, such as ambient light, power requirements, reliability, cost, and so on, must also be taken into account.

On a normal CRT, the characters are produced by reading a character-generation program stored in ROM. Can you explain how the terminal or computer calls on that ROM? If the terminal is intelligent, it performs many of its functions directly, without needing a control program stored in the computer itself, reading signals from the keyboard. Can you show the difference between a "smart" terminal and a "dumb" one, and what a smart terminal's special functions are? There are several strategies for converting the pressing of a key into a signal. Can you explain them?

PAPER OUTPUT

If we want a hard copy of the program or its results, we must have a printer, and that also must be controlled, not just to print characters but to put them in the right places, to advance a line or more, and so on. Some printers can perform rather advanced functions, including reverse line feed, proportional spacing, moving by tiny increments, and so on. Dot printers can produce graphics.

This graphics ability can give a dot printer a decided advantage over formed character printers. Anyone who has tried to type a paper or report using technical or mathematical symbols appreciates the limitations of even a printer with interchangeable printing elements. Although you can easily create special characters with a dot printer, the real problem comes with being able to use these characters when embedded within a text that has been prepared with a word processor. It has been done, but if you develop a similar program that can be used with one of the popular word processing packages, you might have a very valuable product.

It usually is not economical to take a real printer apart to show how it works. Models and diagrams will have to serve you here. A dot printer uses hammers striking wires to construct a matrix of dots on paper. How does this mechanism actually work? A daisy wheel printer works differently; the position of the wheel is mechanically determined, as well as its place on the page. Show how the mechanism works. How does a thermal or electrostatic printer work, and what kind of special paper is needed and why?

The printer receives its instructions from the computer, not only to print a character but also to locate it on the paper. How are these other signals sent without interfering with the character code? Timing is important here, as in other parts of the computer. How does the printer know when to ask for another character? How does the computer know to wait until the printer has finished? Does the printer use a buffer? What is a buffer, how does it work, and why is it desirable?

Although you will need photographs and drawings to supplement this information, you should be able to show each of the functions and operations on the printer itself. If possible, your program should be interactive, but it could be just a demonstration.

MASS STORAGE

The disk drive is, mechanically speaking, the most complicated device home computers have to deal with. Again, a drive you can take apart might not be available to you, but you should be able to provide pictures and diagrams that will show these workings.

A disk drive is called a random-access device, since the information stored on a disk can be retrieved from anywhere without having to read through all the previously stored information. Show how the data is stored, and explain tracks and sectors and formatting. How does the disk head read and write to the disk, and how does it find which track and sector contains the information desired? This is part of the disk's overhead, the reason why a disk might have 120 kilobytes of storage unformatted but only 90 kilobytes formatted. The data stored also contains some of the information needed to retrieve itself. How is this incorporated? Can you write a program (not necessarily a file program) that actually demonstrates how data is written to and read back from a disk?

COMPARISONS AND FEATURES

Any one problem can have different solutions, or programs can be written in more than one way to provide the solution. A comparison of different computers requires different physical machines, but benchmarks can be run comparing different languages, or different programs written to solve the same problem. Can you write a benchmark program that times itself in seconds or machine cycles?

And finally, there are so many makes of computers available today that it is hard to say anything specific that applies to them all. Each make (and model) has its own peculiarities, its own special features and capabilities. These can be demonstrated by showing how they work, and explaining their significance and what special things they enable you to do.

Whatever your interest in science, computers can help. And, in the process of developing your project, you will also learn a lot more about computers.

13

PUTTING IT ALL TOGETHER

In the previous chapters, we've made lots of suggestions that we hope will give you an idea for a project, either for your own purposes or for a science fair. After you've chosen a topic to investigate, or demonstrate, you still have to design that project; that is, you must consider how you are going to do your research, how you will actually perform the experiment, how you will display your results, and so on.

There are several steps you should consider, and if your project is to be entered in a science fair, especially if it is a statewide or national competition, these steps can make the difference between success and failure.

DEFINE YOUR TOPIC

The first and one of the most important things to do is to define your topic and the objective of your project. Just what is it you are going to do? You may start off by deciding that you are going to explore how television works, but that is a rather broad area of investigation. You will want to narrow the idea down somewhat. Are you concerned with the technical problems of broadcasting, the physics of the TV tube, improvements in resolution and image forming, or what?

Even one of these areas, without further refinement, is not specific enough. You should be able to state, in a sentence or two, just what it is you intend your project to do or show when it is finished. You have to know what it is you want to prove, discover, or demonstrate. If your ideas are too broad, you will lack direction and have difficulty with the whole project.

Any idea can serve as a starting point, but it's possible that those that occur to you first have already occurred to other people. You should do a little checking to find out how many others might also be working on a similar topic, or have done so in the past. Even if your topic is not unique, you don't have to give it up—if you can think of a fresh approach, see a question that has been avoided or missed before, or think you have a new solution to an old problem.

You definitely want to avoid doing just another chick embryo experiment. There is still much to be learned from studying chick embryos, but if you go that way you will be hard pressed to produce a project that is not old hat. Since your outlook on the world, and your experience and knowledge, is different from everybody else's, there is a chance that even the most popular of project topics can provide you with a creative and original line of research. But you should familiarize yourself with what is being done and what has been done before to avoid inadvertently duplicating somebody else.

Lots of people like to do something on volcanoes, for instance, since they provide drama in the real world and can be the subject of a dramatic display. If that is your interest, what can you do that will be different or original or creative, and not just a pile of sand with dry ice vapors drifting out of the top?

Explore your rough idea further for interesting variations. After all, there are different kinds of volcanoes, produced by different means. They can be displayed with a model, a cutaway view, in layers, or from the bottom up. They produce not only lava but dust, gas, and ash. Some volcanoes are associated with continental drift, others are not. Related to volcanoes are ocean-floor spreading, mountain-building, and earthquakes. Volcanoes affect the local environment and the global climate. They provide information on how the earth is structured and how it evolves.

Given the initial idea, you can come up with dozens of different special possibilities. List all the variations you can and all the related topics you can think of. Somewhere in the list might be the germ of an original project.

There's a danger in letting your enthusiasm run away with you. The topic you eventually choose must be one that is within your reach. If you know nothing about high-resolution computer graphics, you should not choose that as your topic, at least for this coming science fair. You should already be somewhat knowledgeable about the area of your subject, and it should be one that is of real interest to you. If you pick a topic just because it seems classy or impressive, but have no true interest in it, your lack of enthusiasm will be apparent to all.

You should not only know what your topic is, you should know your goals and how they relate to the field in general and to other fields or applications as well. State the purpose of your project, that is, not only what your topic is but why you are exploring it.

A study of computer use in the neighborhood, no matter how well defined, isn't much good if you don't know why you're doing it. In this case, the purpose might be to show not just that there is a certain percentage of people who have computers but whether ownership is increasing or tapering off. By asking what people do with their computers, you can learn whether they are merely toys or serve truly useful functions in the home. You may wish to show that computer literacy is a problem, or that it isn't.

Of course, you may get results that are contrary to your expectations, but that is a common occurrence—

and a valuable discovery. As you define what your special topic is, then, also keep in mind the reasons why the study should be done, what use it will serve (in addition to satisfying your own curiosity), and what you expect the results of your study to be.

You can think of this, if you like, as practice in preparing research proposals for when you are in college. Obtaining funds for doing serious research is not easy, and the better you are able to express your ideas and the value of the research you intend to do, the greater the chance that such a project will be funded.

MAKE A PLAN

It is a mistake, even with the clearest of ideas in mind, to just dash off and start doing something without a plan. Failure to make a plan causes untold waste in industry and business. You should have a good idea of what steps are necessary for the successful completion of your project— which steps must be done first, which depend on the results of previous steps, and how each step furthers your project.

Designing a project is like writing a structured program. Writing a program without a plan will lead to a large, mossy, buggy program. Doing a science project without a plan will lead to the same kind of result.

It is a good idea to make at least a rough outline of your intended activities. This may be modified over time, as you complete portions and discover problems, but you should endeavor to include everything that pertains to your project.

For example, what research will you have to do? Whom can you ask for help? What equipment might you need, and how or where will you get it? Include shopping and travel time here. How will you prepare your demonstration? Include construction time, and the time necessary to write any software, and to write your report.

These considerations should be arranged in the order in which each step must be taken, rather than in order of importance. Estimate as well as you can how long each step will take, and from that build a timetable. Each step should be as clearly defined as possible, so that you will know when you are supposed to be doing each thing. Bear in mind that you will have only limited time and resources. If, when your first rough outline is finished, it looks like it will take you six months to finish but the deadline is only four months away, you will be able to change your plan, instead of finding yourself suddenly running out of time later.

Besides knowing how much time you will have overall, you should try to figure out how many hours a day you can spend on your project, and how many hours a week. Remember that ideal conditions will seldom exist, so your plan must be flexible to allow for unforeseen events. Have you considered a family trip, the possibility of becoming ill, or the possible difficulty in locating and obtaining certain resources? Allow a reasonable margin for error, but if your project will include activities at which you are inexperienced, such as perhaps building an electronic component, be generous in the time you plan.

You must not only conduct your investigation or experiment, you must also prepare your results for a demonstration. If you finish your analysis of DNA on time, but have no display prepared, you will be out in the cold. You will have to make charts, graphs, perhaps take photographs, write captions, or write a special demonstration program. You will possibly have to write a report and try your demonstration out to make sure it works. All this takes time, and it should be included in your schedule. Plan as much as you can in advance, so that you will know whether or not you are going to meet your deadline.

For many people, now comes a dark moment, when they see just how much work they have ahead of them. It may seem impossible to get so much done in so short a time. In fact, that may be true. Evaluate your plan, per haps with some advice from friends, family, and teachers, to arrive at a realistic idea of whether or not you can actually do the project.

Are there resources that are unavailable, such as Klystron tubes? Have you really bitten off more than you can chew? If your plan is well thought out, based on a good definition of topic and purpose, the chances are you'll have no difficulties, but if the project is unrealistic, now is the time to modify it, not later, when there's only a week left before the fair. You may have to content yourself with a more limited project.

One very important consideration is how much your project will cost. Some projects can be performed and demonstrated using only what you already have, such as your own computer. Some can be done using second-hand, scrap, or surplus parts. Others might require the purchase of new equipment or materials, or that you obtain loans or gifts of some of these. Bear this in mind, so you don't find yourself stymied because you can't afford that plotter or no one will loan you a dot-matrix printer.

This planning will take some time, but it will be time well spent in the long run. After your first rough drafts, draw up a new plan, as if you were preparing it for other people to follow. The act of trying to explain it to others will help clarify your own ideas and may reveal weak points, or unexpected resources.

And now, does your plan really conform to your project definition and purpose, or have you gotten sidetracked along the way? You may have come up with a better idea, in which case you can start over again, but with the advantage of having most of this preparatory work already done. Or you may have gone wrong somewhere and need to revise to bring yourself back in line.

Research proposals also take these considerations into account. A sloppy plan is likely to be turned down, whereas one that is carefully prepared encourages those whose support you are seeking to give you the help you need.

KEEP A NOTEBOOK

If you haven't begun one already, now is a good time to start keeping a notebook. Here is where you will record your plan, your objectives, the results of your work, the citations of your research, and any pertinent thoughts or inspirations. The contents of your notebook will be the foundation for your final report, so the more thorough and careful you are in keeping your notes, the easier it will be to prepare that report.

You may need some advice on the proper way to keep your notebook. Science teachers are good people to ask about this, but you should probably ask more than one, and consult with English teachers as well. You can make your rough notes on anything, but they should then be put into formal form in your regular notebook, keeping track of dates, times of day, citations to works referenced, people met and interviewed, and so on.

Any ideas you have should also be recorded. Don't depend on your memory; it will almost surely fail you. Some of these ideas may be trivial, or beside the point, and they can be edited out later. For this reason, you might want to keep a second, less formal notebook, in which you can write down anything that comes to mind.

And always give credit where it is due. Of course, if you learn something from a book or periodical, you will want to note the title, author, and date for your bibliography. But you should also cite people you interview, TV shows you watch, or even casual conversations or correspondence. Each piece of information should be fully identified, so you can check back on it later.

DO YOUR RESEARCH

The first part of almost any project is research, whether you are knowledgeable already or just a beginner. If you have studied a subject for a long time, much of your research may already be done. But this is a new project you are starting, so more will always be necessary. Doing a project that is just the sum of what you know already will break no new ground. You must expand your knowledge and experience.

Depending on your project and your background, the research may take only a week or two, or it could take months—or years. If you are in junior high, for example, you might start now to think about a project for your senior year, with your current project the first step along the way.

The first place to start your research is to ask your science teacher and other science teachers. If they have had experience with science fairs, or even if they have not, at least one of them will know the area of your topic quite well and can give you practical advice, not only as to how to learn more but how to do the project, whether it is feasible, and how to locate the resources you will need. They can give you hints on how to solve some of your problems, guide you when you go wrong, encourage you when things look dark. Your teachers should always be your first source of inspiration. Even if they can't help you directly, they can steer you to other sources.

Besides your teachers, there may be other people in your town who can help. University professors, scientists and engineers, technicians, and people in industry are all possible sources of information. People usually like to give help, to be able to show how well they know a subject, to share an interest with someone else. Although you must be considerate of their time and other obligations, you shouldn't hesitate to ask experts for help. They will be more likely to give it to you if you can state your objectives clearly and know the questions you need to ask. Your topic definition and plan will be of help here.

But of course, most of your research will be done by reading. Your school library is the first place to start. If there is a junior college, college, or university in your town or nearby, it would be worth the effort to get a card and make use of that library, too. Your public library can be of help. Even small public libraries might have materials you can use.

Don't depend on your familiarity with the stacks or the card catalog. Get to know the reference librarian, and ask advice. That's what he or she is there for, after all. A reference librarian can steer you to books or periodicals you might not think of looking at, or even know exist.

Although there may be books on your chosen subject, periodicals will be even more useful to you. Larger libraries have various indexes of periodical literature, and some periodicals publish their own indexes. Again, the librarian can be of considerable help here. Sometimes, for example, there may be no book on the particular subject you are interested in, such as the uses of computers in space science. In that case, articles in periodicals and magazines may be your sole source of printed information.

There are many journals devoted to special topics, such as computer graphics, petroleum chemistry, or animal breeding. Most of these are written for people who are already experts in the field, and may be way over your head. Some of them, however, give bibliographies at the end of the article or report, giving you leads for new places to search.

Another place where source materials are listed is an encyclopedia. Encyclopedias in themselves can be a good place to start. Don't depend on only the main entry, however; check the index for cross references.

A number of popular magazines can also be helpful, such as *Scientific American, Science Digest, Science News, Smithsonian, Psychology Today, Technology Illustrated,* and so on. Some of these are more reliable than others, so you should always read with a skeptical eye, especially if the magazine seems somewhat sensationalistic. Even with the best of intentions and high integrity, however, new research can be misreported, premature, or of doubtful relevance. This is especially true of science reported in newspapers, where "startling new facts" are sometimes written of by people who have no understanding of the subject. Double-check anything that seems doubtful, or too good to be true.

And be careful of any information that is more than a few years old. Books and periodicals can and do go out of date. Some laws, data, or theories remain valid for decades or centuries, but in certain areas new knowledge replaces the old both quickly and often; this is especially true in computer science.

DO THE WORK

Of course, you must eventually actually perform the experiment, make the observation, construct the device, do the project. In fact, the sooner you get started, the better. It is a mistake to try to do all your research first, because research never ends. The project itself is the main element in your plan, and only by beginning to work on it will you learn whether you've done enough research or need to do more.

As you do the project, there are two kinds of problems you may encounter. The first is that a side issue becomes so fascinating that you lose track of your main objective. By all means make note of such peripheral details and questions, as they may prove useful later or may provide you with another project for another time. But never lose sight of what it is you are trying to do. Stick to your plan.

Unless the second problem arises. You may find that someone else has already done what you are trying to do, or that the project is trivial, or that it is too complicated and beyond your capabilities. In that case you will have to change your tack, to find a new approach or a more meaningful question to ask, or to limit the scope of your endeavors. This is not an uncommon problem in the real world.

WRITE A REPORT

The last thing you may need to do, aside from setting up your display, is to write a report on what you have done and how you did it. You will have to check with the science fair advisers on the proper form for this, of course. It is here that you wil find that the effort you spent in maintaining your notebook will pay off.

PREPARE YOUR DISPLAY

You will probably be considering your display from the earliest stages of your work. Depending on the facilities available and the recommendations of the science fair adviser, there will be limitations as to the size of the display, the availability of electricity, lighting, and so on. You should check out these limitations and constraints beforehand, to avoid the disappointment of creating a truly wonderful display that won't fit in the space available.

If you have used your computer only to solve problems, analyze data, or prepare charts and graphs, you will have no special worries, but if a computer is to be a part of your display, you may have to make additional preparations. First find out whether computers will actually be allowed. Then determine what power supply you will need and what is available. You may want to include a voltage regulator to protect the computer from power peaks or brownouts.

If you are going to be shipping your computer, you must make sure that it will arrive in exactly the same shape in which you sent it. If you have kept the original cartons, that will help. Large equipment, such as printers and monitors, can present a problem, and these must be considered. Also, can you do without your computer while it's at the fair?

We've mentioned the importance of a good display or demonstration many times in this book, but you should give special consideration to just what aspects of your work you wish to show. Unnecessary detail should be avoided. What you want to do is communicate to people, and to judges, just what your project is and what you have accomplished. Here you can refer to the definition of your topic and statement of purpose, so that the point of your work is what you actually get across.

FOR SPECIAL CONSIDERATION

If you are not familiar with science fairs, you should try to attend one. See what the other students have done, to help you gauge whether your idea is up to their standards or whether it might be too ambitious. Take careful note of how each project is displayed, especially when it comes to computer display.

If your school does not conduct science fairs, some teacher is sure to know how to find out which schools nearby do. You can write to Science Service, Inc., the coordinating body that directs science fairs across the country and around the world, for more information. Their address is 1719 N Street, N.W., Washington, D.C. 20036.

In Chapter 1, we suggested the possibility of collaborating with a partner. This does not always work, and sometimes is not allowed. You should check with your science fair adviser, the school rules, and other rules that may apply. Teams sometimes fail because one person just rides along on the expertise and efforts of the others. With computers, however, there is still a strong possibility, if it is allowed, that two persons can successfully collaborate, especially if one is a computer expert and the other is expert in the subject of the project. Consult with your advisers first, in any event.

INDEX

Acceleration, 64ff., 83
Acoustics, 50
Airfoils, 68
Analog information, 28–29, 83
Animation. See Graphics
Apples, 4
Artificial intelligence, 106
Artificial language, 18–19
Astronomy, 57, 67. See also Stars
Ataris, 4

Ballistics, 66
Bar graphs, 59, 60
Bases, number, 25–26
BASIC, 14, 23, 37, 38, 97, 98, 120–26
Border patterns, 43
Business, 16, 59–60

Calculus, 56
Chance, 21–22
Charts. See Graphs and charts
Chess, 102
Clouds, 72–73
Coal, 41
COBOL, 13–14, 98
Color, 85–86
    and light, 55–56

Colorado River, 47
Comparative programming, 95–97
Conic sections, 56–57
Continental drift, 45ff.
CRTs, 103–7
Crystals, 48

Data analysis, 28–35
Data files, 13–14ff., 25, 33
Deaf, the, 54
Demographic studies, 33–35
Digital information, 83. See also Data analysis
Dithering, 86
Doubled-precision calculators, 26

Earth, 29–31
    structure of, 45–67
Earthquakes, 29–30
Ecology, 75–76
Economics, 78–80
Eigen, Manfred, 78, 127
ELIZA, 100
Encyclopedias, 116
Energy, 70–71
Escape codes, 39
Evolution, 73–75

Flowcharts, 11–12, 95, 96
Forecasting. *See* Simulation and modeling
FORTH, 38, 97
FORTRAN, 23, 98
Fruit flies, 73–74

Game of Life, 76ff., 128
Games, 83, 100–1, 127–28. *See also* specific games
Genetics, 73–75
Geometry, 40
Geosynclines, 47
Go, 128
Grand Canyon, 97
Graphics, 2, 36–37. *See also* Graphs and charts
  pictorial representation, 33–57
Graphs and charts, 58–63, 79
Gravity. *See* Simulation and modeling
Greenhouse Effect, 72

Handicapped persons, 53–55
Heat pumps, 71
Housing, 70–71

Information, 9–10
  manipulation, 13–19
Input, 103

Joysticks, 84

Knot theory, 57

Languages, 94–96. *See also* Writing
  artificial, 18–19
  artist's, 38. *See also* Graphics
Laws of the Game, 78, 127–28
LCDs, 104

Letter frequencies, 18
Lemonade Stand, 78–80
Library, 115–16
Light and color, 55–56
Line graphs, 61–62
LISP, 98
Logic, 56
LOGO, 37, 40, 98
Lunar Lander, 65–67

Magazines, 116
Mass storage, 106
Mathematics, *See also* Graphs and charts; Simulation and modeling
  art of, 56–59
  of art, 39–41
Mean deviation, 31–32
Medicine, 151
Meteorology. *See* Weather
Minerals, solid, 47–48
Mississippi River, 47
Molecules, in motion, 48–50
Money, 78–80
Monitors, 93
Music, 88–90
Mutations, 73ff.

Neighborhoods, 76–78
Notebooks, 114, 116
Numerical calculation, 20, 27. *See also* Mathematics

Office design, 52–53
Ozone, 73

P41, 23
Panagaea, 45, 46
Parsecs, 24
Partners, 119
Pascal, 97, 98
PEI, 4
Pictorial representation, 44–57
Pie charts, 59

Pixels and patterns, 41–43
Plan, making, 111–13
Plate tectonics, 45ff.
Player/missiles, 37
Politics, 80
Polls, 33–35
Prehistoric artifacts, 50–51
Printing, 101–6
Probability, 31, 32
Programs (programming), 94–99
    coordinate conversion, 120–26
Psychology, 85, 87

Reading, 53–55
Report, writing, 118
Researching, 114–17
Rivers, 47
Robots and robotics, 6, 82
ROM, 104
Room design, 52–53
Routines and subroutines, 21–23

Scale, 68, 70
Scatter diagrams, 59–62
Science, graphics and, 51–52
Science Service Inc., 119
Self-operating program, 6
Shape, 85–86
Sign language, 54
Simulation and modeling, 64–8, 92ff.

Solar heat, 70–71
Sound, 50, 86, 88–91
Speed, 83
Sprites, 37–39
Stars, 23–25, 94–95
Statistics, 31–32, 33–35
Stonehenge, 50–51
Supplementary materials, 11–12
Surveys, 33–35

Teachers, 115, 119
TI-99/4A, 4
Time, 83, 87
Timex/Sinclair 1000, 4
Topological studies, 57
Traffic patterns, 52–53
Trains, model, 82
Trigonometry, 23, 26, 56
TRS-80, 4
Turtle graphics, 40–41

Underground houses, 71

Velocity, 83
VIC-20, 4
Voice, 90–91
Volcanoes, 36–37, 72, 109–110

Weather, 62–63, 71–73
Whispering galleries, 50
Winkler, Ruthild, 78, 137
Word processing, 17–18
Writing, 17–18

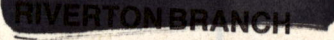